Tournament Poker
for Advanced Players
Expanded Edition

By
David Sklansky

A product of Two Plus Two Publishing LLC
www.twoplustwo.com

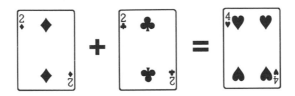

THIRD EDITION

FIRST PRINTING
DECEMBER 2007

Printing and Binding
Creel Printing Co.
Las Vegas, Nevada

Printed in the United States of America

Tournament Poker
for Advanced Players
Expanded Edition

COPYRIGHT © 2002, 2003, 2007 David Sklansky
and Two Plus Two Publishing LLC

For information contact: **Two Plus Two Publishing LLC**
32 Commerce Center Drive
Suite H-89
Henderson, NV 89014
www.twoplustwo.com

ISBN: 1-880685-41-8
ISBN13: 978-1-880685-41-9

To Dr. Jack Henri Vitenson

The Best Urologist in America

Thanks for giving me all
the extra years with my dad.

Table of Contents

About David Sklansky

David Sklansky is generally considered the number one authority on gambling in the world today. Besides his twelve books on the subject, David also has produced two videos and numerous writings for various gaming publications. His occasional poker seminars always receive an enthusiastic reception, including those given at the Taj Mahal in Atlantic City and the World Series of Poker in Las Vegas.

More recently, David has been doing consulting work for casinos, Internet gaming sites, and gaming device companies. He has recently invented several games, soon to appear in casinos.

David attributes his standing in the gambling community to three facts:

1. The fact that he presents his ideas as simply as possible (sometimes with Mason Malmuth) even though these ideas frequently involve concepts that are deep, subtle, and not to be found elsewhere.

2. The fact that David's teachings have proven to be accurate.

3. The fact that to this day a large portion of his income is still derived from gambling (usually poker, but occasionally blackjack, sports betting, horses, video games, casino promotions, or casino tournaments).

Thus, those who depend on David's advice know that he still depends on it himself.

Other Books by David Sklansky

Hold 'em Poker
The Theory of Poker
Getting The Best of It
Sklansky on Poker
Poker, Gaming, & Life
Sklansky Talks Blackjack

Gambling for a Living by David Sklansky and Mason Malmuth
Hold 'em Poker for Advanced Players by David Sklansky and Mason Malmuth
Seven-Card Stud for Advanced Players by David Sklansky, Mason Malmuth, and Ray Zee
Small Stakes Hold 'em: Winning Big with Expert Play by Ed Miller, David Sklansky, and Mason Malmuth
No-Limit Hold 'em: Theory and Practice by David Sklansky and Ed Miller

Introduction

When I started playing poker for a living, poker tournaments did not exist. Then about 35 years ago, the Horseshoe Casino in Las Vegas came up with an idea which they called the World Series of Poker. This event offered a poker tournament every other day, as well as incredible high stakes side action. For many years, the only poker tournament (actually a collection of tournaments) was, in fact, the World Series of Poker. The final event was a $10,000 no-limit hold 'em tournament. The winner of that tournament was crowned the World Champion of Poker. Thirty-five some years later, the winner of that tournament is still regarded by most people as the World Champion.

A few years after the World Series of Poker started, a small number of other casinos decided to offer their own collection of tournaments. These included Amarillo Slim's Super Bowl of Poker, originally held at Lake Tahoe, and the Stairway to the Stars Poker Tournament held at the Stardust in Las Vegas. Like the World Series of Poker, they had a final event that cost $5,000 or $10,000 to enter, and a series of smaller events that usually cost between $300 and $2,000. This was the tournament situation for quite a few years; three or four major events, including the World Series of Poker, that broke up the monotony of the day-to-day games that serious poker players had to endure.

Then about ten years ago, poker tournaments exploded in their availability. Those who preferred tournaments over side games could find a decent sized tournament to play almost any day of the year. Some, in fact, chose to do just that, traveling around the country, playing in event after event. (Other professional poker players also followed the "tournament trail," not to play in the events themselves, but to play in the "side games" that spring up around the tournaments.) In fact, tournaments have now become so popular that small buy-in events (usually between $20-to-$100) are a common feature of many cardrooms.

More recently this popularity has exploded. Starting in 2003, the World Poker Tour tournaments made their debut and something very unique happened. Not only were these tournaments televised, but through the use of an ingenious "lipstick" camera, all player's hands were shown and no-limit hold'em tournaments quickly became a worldwide sensation with an avalanche of new players, many of whom played on the Internet, entering our field.

With this happening, poker, and of course poker tournaments, reached a level of popularity that was never anticipated. Now poker tournaments are even more widespread. Between the Internet and brick and mortar cardrooms you can play a serious tournament for significant money at any time in any location, and this popularity is now worldwide.

But there is one more unique characteristic of this tournament boom. It is the fact that no-limit hold 'em became the feature game. "I'm all-in" is now a common expression not only in cardrooms but almost everyplace else. Poker has hit the big time and no-limit hold 'em tournaments are now the featured game even though there are still many tournaments for the other forms of poker, and of course there are still lots of side games.

The question, of course, is whether there is good money to be made playing tournaments. The short answer is yes. There is no doubt that the better players have a definite long run edge (or what gamblers call a positive EV). Furthermore, this edge is significant, and can add up to a lot of money, as long as the buy-in is substantial. There are, however, three major downsides to concentrating on tournament play for your livelihood. They are:

1. There is great volatility to your short term results. If, for example, you are good enough to win a 100 player tournament once every 40 tries, on average, you still can go an awful long time before you get that win.

2. To be a serious tournament player requires a willingness to travel all over the country, or even the world. This is especially true if you are interested in playing the largest buy-in tournaments. However, some locales now offer many smaller tournaments, and this is true of many Internet poker sites as well.

3. When you play in a tournament, you cannot play in a regular ring game. There are many players who can beat tournaments who would still be better off in the long run playing in a normal game.

In spite of the three aforementioned downsides, the fact is that serious poker players should, at least occasionally, consider playing in a poker tournament. Not only because of the positive EV involved, but also because of the chance of a score, and the fact that a change of routine can never hurt once in awhile. But if you are going to play in a tournament, it stands to reason you should play that tournament as well as possible. Most good players don't. That is what this book is for.

So what exactly will this book show you? It will explain how your play should differ when in a tournament from how you play in a regular game. Most other books that have attempted to do that are either flawed or incomplete.[1] This book will show you exactly where strategy changes, compared to normal games, are indicated, and why.

What this book will not do, however, is teach you how to play good poker. It assumes that you already do that. The changes that you make in a tournament won't help you much if you don't already play well. If you are not yet at that level where you can

---

[1] I do recommend the three *Harrington on Hold 'em* books by Dan Harrington and Bill Robertie which are also published by Two Plus Two Publishing LLC. They were produced after the original edition of this text. So my statement is still accurate.

beat medium sized poker games, you need to study *The Theory of Poker, Hold 'em Poker for Advanced Players, Seven-Card Stud for Advanced Players, High-Low-Split Poker for Advanced Players, No-Limit Hold 'em: Theory and Practice,* and other appropriate books published by Two Plus Two Publishing LLC.

If you already play well, you would probably show a small long run profit making absolutely no adjustments for the fact that you are in a tournament. The reason being that most of the other players don't play as well as you. However, your failure to make adjustments will cost you a lot of money.

Finally, I would like to express my appreciation to Dr. Alan Schoonmaker for assisting in the editing of this work. Thanks to him, my ideas are now more clearly stated and thus should be more easily understood.

Introduction
to the Expanded Edition

The first edition of this book was written just before no-limit hold 'em tournaments exploded on the scene. At that time, it would have been inappropriate to have put undue emphasis on this form of poker in my discussion of tournaments.

That's because the majority of tournaments (at that time) were not no-limit. In fact, many of them weren't even hold 'em. The tournament format proved to be a good format for many different forms of poker, (some of which were only rarely spread as ring games), and no-limit hold 'em, while popular as a tournament game, was only one of these forms. Today, however, it is the dominant form.

In fact, just a few years ago, no-limit hold 'em was hardly spread anywhere as a ring game. Limit hold 'em was the game followed by a fair amount of seven-card stud. No-limit hold 'em was mainly for tournaments. Of course, all of that has changed. No-limit hold 'em is currently the main game whether it is a tournament or a side game.

In addition, while there were always tournaments to play, there certainly weren't as many. Now-a-days it seems like you can always be playing in a tournament. And this isn't only because of the rise of Internet poker where tournaments are offered at all hours and all levels of buy-ins. Our brick and mortar cardrooms are offering many more tournaments than before in an attempt to satisfy their customer demand.

So now that things have changed and the previous edition has sold out, we felt it was a good idea to add quite a bit of new material specifically devoted to no-limit hold 'em. If you already have the original edition of *Tournament Poker for Advanced*

Players and you think that it isn't worth paying an extra thirty bucks for 101 new pages, that is your decision. But it's a bad one.

I want to thank Charmaine Malmuth for her help with my dictation and proof reading. She's the fastest typist I've ever seen. I also need to thank Mason Malmuth for reviewing all this material and for his many comments. We think this book is now just about as good as it can be.

Also, a big thank-you to Jason "Gonso" Hughes for his great cover design. Not only does it look great, but it is now easily the best looking cover in the *for Advanced Players* series.

And finally, I need to thank Two Plus Two Publishing LLC. It's a great organization and I'm proud to be a part of it.

Using This Book

This book is a little different from other books in the *for Advanced Players* series in that it assumes you already know how to play poker well. If that's not the case, you will need to read and study those titles mentioned in the "Introduction."

But if you already have a good understanding of how to play poker well and want to expand into tournament poker, this is certainly the book along with the *Harrington on Hold 'em* series to study. However, although I say study, it is recommended that the whole book be read first, after which you can return to those sections that require more effort.

Once you feel that your understanding of this material is fairly complete, you should then concentrate on the "Hand Quizzes." Having a good understanding of proper tournament strategy and being able to implement it "in the heat of battle," are not always the same thing. The quizzes will help in this area and many of you will find it to be the most important part of the book.

As with all forms of poker, I don't recommend that you immediately buy in to a large limit event. Even though the strategies in this book are designed with these events in mind, it is still better to start lower and work your way up. However, if you enter and win a low cost satellite that puts you in one of these events, I certainly have no problem with that.

Keep in mind, as the text emphasizes, that proper poker tournament strategy and proper side game strategy are sometimes very different. For example, it might be that a hand which should be played for a raise in a side game, should be mucked in a tournament. One of the keys to successful tournament play is to recognize these situations and make the appropriate adjustments, even if it doesn't (at first) feel quite right.

Note: Cards designated in the text are either underlined or not. If a card is underlined, then it is a hole card in a stud hand;

otherwise it is either an upcard or not part of a stud hand. For example, if you see A♣A♠ and we are talking about hold 'em, this is representing a starting hand of two black aces. If you see A♣A♠A♥, then this is a starting stud hand of three aces and the two black aces are down.

Why Play Tournament Poker?

To reiterate, this book is written for someone who has a good understanding of standard ring game poker. Assuming that's the case, you will already be winning at the poker table. So why venture into the tournament arena?

The answer is easy. As I stated in the "Introduction," there is good money to be made in tournaments; there is a chance for a big score; and a change in routine can keep you fresh.

You win at tournament poker because of two important factors. First, some of your opponents play poker badly, and in extreme cases literally give their money away. This includes players who consistently lose in side games, and now, perhaps out of frustration, want to give tournaments a shot. In most cases, their results will be the same.

The second reason you can win money playing tournaments is because this form of poker will offer numerous opportunities for the expert player to make adjustments from standard side game strategy. Many of your opponents, even those who play poker fairly well, do not understand what these adjustments are, or fail to implement them correctly. This will sometimes cause them to make serious errors, especially late in an event, which you can take advantage of.

I mentioned earlier that the risk factor in tournaments is very high. That is "there is great volatility to your short term results."[2] You may also need to travel, and when in a tournament, you can't play a ring game. So tournaments, especially on a day-in and day-out basis, are not for everyone.

---

[2] See my book *Poker, Gaming, & Life* for more discussion.

Nonetheless, besides their long term profitability they can be very exciting to play. This is especially true when you have reached the final table and so much is riding on the turn of a card.

So given the tremendous growth of poker tournaments, and the fact that they are here to stay, there's no reason not to join in. They may or may not be right for you everyday, but they can certainly be worth your time on occasion. And who knows, perhaps the next poker show that is shown worldwide will feature you at the final table.

Part One
Getting Started

Getting Started

Introduction

Before you play a poker tournament you need to know how a tournament works and how it differs from a side game. We'll see that if you have chips, you can't quit (unless you manage to get them all) and if you run out of chips, you must quit (assuming you are not in what is known as the rebuy period that some tournaments offer). In addition, we'll see that winning all the chips does not get you all the money, and that you might still win a substantial prize even though you have lost every chip that you started with.

But most important, I'll start to talk about how these factors not only impact your strategy, but how they frequently affect the way your opponents play, which should also impact your strategy. As already mentioned, not only are tournaments different from standard poker, but proper tournament *strategy* can be quite a bit different as well.

How a Poker Tournament Works

I assume that most people who are reading this book are very familiar with the rules of poker tournaments, so this will be short and sweet. If you are not, there are many other sources where more detailed information is available.

In a typical tournament, everyone enters for the same amount of money, say $500. The house usually charges an extra "entry fee," say $30, which they pocket. The total prize pool, comprised of the $500 buy-ins are distributed to the winner, second place, third place, down to whatever the rules of the tournament specify. (Often 18, 20, or more places on occasion.[3]) If, for example, this tournament had 200 entries, there would be a $100,000 total prize pool. At the beginning of the tournament, each player would receive $500 in chips. (Sometimes the non-negotiable chips have a face value different from the actual buy-in, but that is of no consequence, and is readjusted at the end of the tournament.)

Usually a tournament involves just one game. It may be limit hold 'em, no-limit hold 'em, seven-card stud, or Omaha high-low-split eight-or-better. Occasionally, the tournament involves multiple games that are changed after a specified time period. The stakes start out fairly small in comparison to the buy-in. In the $500 example, they may start out at the $10-$20 or $15-$30 level. With 200 entries there might be twenty ten handed tables, all playing those stakes. As time goes by, the stakes are raised. Typically, they are raised once an hour. In the example given, the second hour might be $20-$40, followed by $30-$60, $50-$100, $75-$150, $100-$200, etc. Players who go broke are eliminated.

---

[3] In the 2006 World Series of Poker $10,000 main event, over 800 places were paid.

(There are some tournaments that allow a player who goes broke to buy in again during a specified time period early in the tournament. The principles discussed in this book will assume generally that the tournament is either not a rebuy tournament or that you have passed the point where rebuys are allowed. There will, however, be a short chapter discussing how this aspect of tournaments should be handled.)

As players go broke, tables are broken up and combined. (Most well run tournaments break up tables in a pre-specified order. Knowing when your table will be broken up can be helpful to your tournament strategy, as we will discuss later).

The tournament does not end until one person has all the chips. In the old days, that person won everything. He would have walked away with $100,000 in our example. Later on casinos realized that they were much better off spreading the money around. They experimented briefly with stopping the tournament when a certain number of players were left, and letting those players keep what they had in front of them. For instance, they might stop this particular tournament when five players were left, and the winner would be the one who had the most chips, maybe $40,000, fifth place would have the least chips, maybe $1,500, and everybody would keep what they had. Tournaments like that are extremely rare nowadays. They require a somewhat different strategy and will not be discussed in this book

The way tournaments are paid off now works like this: Once again, the tournament does not end until one player has all the chips. However, that player no longer wins all the money. Instead, the casino makes note of what point each player becomes eliminated, and pays off based on that. The last player to be eliminated wins second prize, the next to last player wins third prize, and so on. In most tournaments, prizes are awarded to everyone who makes the last table. Those tournaments with many entries often award prizes to those who make it to the next to last table. The World Series of Poker final event, because it has so many entries, pays players at many tables. The prizes are a pre-specified percentage of the total prize money. For example, if this $500 tournament was a hold 'em tournament that paid ten places, first prize might be 30 percent of the total prize pool, second prize might be 20 percent, followed by 13, 10, 7, 6, 5, 4, 3, and 2 percent respectively. (In larger tournaments, the smallest payments might be less than 1 percent.) If two people were eliminated simultaneously they would share their prizes, or in some tournaments, the larger prize would go to the player who started that hand with more chips.

How Poker
Tournaments are Different

There are many reasons why you cannot simply play your normal, tough poker strategy and expect to extract the maximum amount from a poker tournament. The fact is that poker tournaments are different from regular games. How they are different and what that means for your optimum strategy will be discussed in detail in subsequent chapters. For now, I just want to list these differences.

1. You must quit if you lose what you have in front of you.

2. They must quit if they lose what they have in front of them.

3. The stakes are constantly raised. (Thus, "advertising" plays can reap bigger rewards than usual).

4. You will often be faced with situations in which you or your opponent is "all-in" before all of the cards are out.

5. Your table will be broken up, and in many tournaments you will know about when that will happen.

6. When you have a very short stack, you must consider whether you can afford to wait for a normally good starting hand.

7. Hourly rate considerations do not apply.

8. Other players' stack sizes have great significance, especially at the end of a tournament.

9. Hands played between other opponents are very significant, even when you are not in that hand.

10. Because of the way prizes are distributed, your goals differ from what they would be in a regular game. For example, in theory, you could finish second place without ever having more chips than you started with.

EV

Many times in this book I will use the term EV. It is an abbreviation for the words *expected value*. Every bet has an expected value, either positive, negative, or zero. Basically, expected value means the amount you will win or lose per bet if you could somehow make it a large number of times.

For instance, if someone stupidly offered you $300-to-$200 on a flip of a coin, you have an expected value of positive $50. Why? Because after many such bets you would be ahead an average of $50 per bet. Had you made 10 bets, you would average winning five and losing five, putting you up $500, or $50 per bet.

$$\$500 = (5)(\$300) - (5)(\$200)$$

$$\$50 = \left(\frac{\$500}{10} \right)$$

If someone offered you $1,320-to-$200, against your rolling a seven with two dice, you figure to win $1,320 one time, while losing $200 five times. (Since rolling seven is a 1-in-6 shot [or 5-to-1 against.)] That puts you up $320 after six times, which is a positive EV of $53.33.

$$\$320 = (1)(\$1,320) - (5)(\$200)$$

$$53.33 = \frac{\$329}{6}$$

So the dice bet has a higher expected value than the coin flip bet, and would usually be the one you would take if you could only take one.

It is not necessary that the EV of a bet can be calculated so precisely in order for it to be thought of in those terms. For instance, when playing $10-20 hold 'em, we could speculate on what the EV of a pair of aces on the button is. Depending on the game and your skill level, I would suspect that it is around $60.

We could also speculate on the EV of two alternate plays with the same hand. What is the EV of calling with:

under-the-gun, as compared with the EV of raising with it from the same position? (Folding has an obvious EV of zero.)

In all of these cases we are simply talking about the average amount per hand you will win (or lose) if you were to play the hand that way many times in the same situation. Experienced players will have a good idea as to what these numbers truly are, and they can play an important part in your overall winning strategy.

In this book, EV is mentioned frequently because it turns out that in a tournament it is not always right to choose the play with the slightly higher EV. This is because the higher EV bet may be more likely to lose. In the dice example, your $53.33 EV came with a bet that would lose five-sixths of the time. The $50 EV coin flip bet involved something that would lose only half the time. Assuming that you have enough money to withstand short-term fluctuations, it is always better to choose the bet with the higher EV. But if you do not have that cushion, it may well be right to choose the slightly smaller EV if that bet will win more often, especially if going broke keeps you from making more positive EV bets.

Notice, that may well be your situation in a poker tournament. Balancing your quest for extra EV and your quest for survival is a major factor in proper tournament strategy. In a side game, this will not be a major consideration since you should almost always have enough money to keep playing (even if you have to reach into your pocket for more). That will often not be the case in a tournament, and we will shortly see that some of those standard side game plays that you are used to making are not always correct at the tournament table.

You're Broke
— You're Done

Aside from the early stages of a rebuy tournament, the fact is that losing all your chips is worse in a tournament than it is in a regular game. There are two reasons for this. One has to do with the way tournaments are paid. Your prize money depends solely on the point at which you were eliminated, not how much you had when you were eliminated. Thus, it is especially catastrophic to go broke when only a few people are left. For instance, suppose four players are left, you have the second largest amount of chips and get busted by the chip leader. You come in fourth, while the other two players move up in standings simply by watching you lose your money.

We will have more to say later about the proper strategy for the times you make the last table, but for now you can see that in situations like this, there is a great incentive to avoid going broke, especially with debatable, mildly profitable hands. To give an extreme example, suppose on the last day of the $10,000 No-Limit Hold 'em World Championship at the World Series of Poker there were four players left, the two shortest stacks had about $30,000 each, you had $200,000 and the leader was sitting on millions of dollars of chips. Suppose you foolishly played against that big chip leader and lost everything. That cost you perhaps as much as several million dollars in prize money considering that you could have probably antied your way into second place.

The above factor (which would indicate that you avoid close gambles with a slight advantage, to keep from going broke) only takes on significance near the very end of a tournament. But there is another reason to eschew close gambles even early on. This reason has nothing to do with the prize structure, and in fact is something you should be aware of even if the tournament paid only one winner. What I am speaking of involves the presumption that you are one of the best players in the tournament. That being the case, you should avoid close gambles, especially for large portions of your chips. It may seem that giving up a positive EV gamble can never be right. However, even from a purely mathematical standpoint, you sometimes should.

For instance, suppose I knew that tomorrow someone would offer me $200-to-$100 on a coin flip. Meanwhile, today someone offers me $120-to-$100 on a coin flip. The problem is that I only have $100 to my name, and will not be able to play tomorrow if I lose today. If I take the first bet, I will miss out on the opportunity for the second bet half the time.

If I take the first bet, along with the second bet if I have the money, I will be broke half the time, I will have profited $20 one-fourth of the time, and profited $320 the other fourth of the time. That is a positive EV of $35.

$$\$35 = \left(\frac{1}{2}\right)(-\$100) + \left(\frac{1}{4}\right)(\$20) + \left(\frac{1}{4}\right)(\$320)$$

If instead I wait until tomorrow, I'll be broke half the time and end up $200 ahead the other half. That is an EV of $50.

$$\$50 = \left(\frac{1}{2}\right)(-\$100) + \left(\frac{1}{2}\right)(\$200)$$

So you can see that it can be mathematically correct to pass up a good bet if losing that bet can keep you from making an even better bet later on.

There are two different ways this can apply to poker situations.

One, you have a heads-up situation with a hand that is only barely worth playing EV wise. For example, playing no-limit hold 'em, if a player moves all-in with what you somehow know is you would seriously consider throwing away

getting barely above even money, if losing that pot would get you broke or near broke. This, in spite of the fact that a pair of fours is a tiny favorite over ace-king suited.

Other close heads-up situations that you might opt to fold would involve getting pot odds that are just a tad above that which you need to give you a positive EV. In other words, you might not take 4.3-to-1 on a 4-to-1 shot. Since saving a bet gives you more ammunition.

A more important example of this concept involves choosing whether to play a hand multiway as opposed to heads-up or short handed. Put another way, you may have a decision whether to slowplay a good hand. Well, once again assuming you are one of the best players in the tournament, the answer is that most prospective slowplays should not be made. Unless you have a "monster" hand, slowplaying, while often making you more when it works, entails an extra risk of losing the pot. This risk is often worth taking in a regular game, but not in a tournament.

To give a mathematical example, suppose you could choose either to get 100-to-20 odds on a 75 percent shot, or 80-to-40 odds on a 90 percent shot. If you work it out, you will see that the first situation gives you an EV of $70, while the second one gives you an EV of $68.

$$70 = (.75)(100) - (.25)(20)$$

$$68 = (.90)(80) - (.10)(40)$$

However, the second one gives you only a 10 percent chance of losing, while the first one, has a 25 percent chance of losing. Therefore, that second one gives you an extra 15 percent chance of not only losing that $20, but also the $80 that you could have won. It is almost definitely worth giving up $2 in EV to avoid this disaster in a poker tournament. Notice that this example is equivalent to suggesting that you raise $20 and get two calls, compared to calling $20 and getting five calls. Situations like this come up all the time. Slowplaying in these situations is often wrong, even early in the tournament (when you are a top player), and almost definitely wrong late in a tournament.[4]

Please do not misunderstand what I am saying here. My point is that, if you are one of the best players in the tournament, you should usually not risk significant money on very close decisions. But those decisions must be close. (Also, as we will soon see, the decisions I am speaking of involve situations where someone else has already bet.) If it's close, fold hands where calls might be a very slight positive EV, and raise (if that will knock players out) where a slowplaying call might have a very slightly higher EV. But again, remember, that these strategy deviations, especially early in the tournament, assume you are one of the best players in the tournament.

There are also quite a few exceptions to the above. Here are some reasons why you might choose *not* to stay away from close decisions:

---

[4] Yet in a side game where you can always reach into your pocket for more money, this exact same play is usually absolutely correct.

1. There is a juicy side game that you would love to play in if
    you get knocked out of the tournament. Obviously, in a case
    like this, your inclination would be to either quickly increase
    your stack, or to go broke. If that is so, you would not only be
    glad to risk significant tournament chips with a slight edge,
    you might even want to do it with a disadvantage.

2. Hourly rate means something to you. We will go into this
    further in another chapter. Simply put, tournament players are
    not usually concerned about their hourly rate. They just want
    to maximize their average profit per tournament. This is
    different from their average profit per hour played in the
    tournament. But if for some reason, your hourly rate in the
    tournament matters, (usually because there is another
    tournament or side game you'll get into if you go broke) then
    avoiding close gambles, when you have a little bit the best of
    it, may no longer be worth doing.

3. You are concerned about your future image. Any time you
    can deceive your opponents at lower stakes to the point
    where they will make a mistake against you once the stakes
    are raised, you gain a lot from that deception. Thus, you may
    not want to tip off your opponents early on that you are
    avoiding close gambles, lest they take advantage of that later
    on when the stakes have increased.

4. You may want to take high pot odds with a bit the worst of it.
    The idea of avoiding close gambles to reduce your chances

of going broke doesn't really apply to situations in which your risk is small. For instance, seeing the flop with

getting debatable odds. There are certain psychological and technical advantages to significantly increasing your stack early on, and as long as your EV is not really negative and your risk is small, this could be a gamble worth taking.

5. You have the smallest stack at the last table. There will be a full chapter on last table strategy. For now, understand that when you have the smallest stack, most of your opponents will be playing conservatively, hoping you go broke, which will move them up the prize ladder. Because of this, you must take chances, since your only real hope is to get lucky somewhere along the line. (Keep in mind however, that this concept totally reverses if other smaller stacks are foolishly playing too loosely. In that case the principles of this chapter would hold even more than usual. In other words, in a situation like that, you would stay away from any gamble even remotely close, so that it would be you who moves up the prize ladder.)

6. Again, the avoidance of gambles mentioned in this chapter relates to when someone else has bet. When you are the original bettor or raiser, you will not play *fewer* hands than you would in a normal game, but in fact, most likely play *more*. The reason, as we will see next chapter, is that your opponents are probably just as worried as you are about going broke.

Note: So far, everything written in this chapter is based upon the premise that you are one of the better players in the tournament, and since you're reading this book, that will most likely be the case. But this assumption isn't necessarily true. It just might be that your tournament skills are lacking, and when this is the case, how do you approach those close gambles?

First off, you need to realize that there are two common situations where your poker tournament skills may be deficient. The first occurs when you are relatively new to tournaments. Like many aspects of poker, experience is important, and this is certainly true here. The second situation occurs when you're at a tough table that won't be broken for a while. While this won't be the norm, tough tables do occur, especially after part of the field has been eliminated.

So what should you do when this is the case? The obvious answer is to now embrace those close gambles and take a few chances. If you get lucky, you'll be in good shape. If you're not successful, there's a good chance you would have been ground down anyway.[5]

However, don't use this bit of advice as an excuse to play recklessly. Sometimes poker players will seize on erroneous information to make creative plays. So don't take these close gambles unless you are sure you have the worst of it and that you are clearly against superior opponents.

---

[5] For more discussion, see "When Will Your Table Break-Up" starting on page 59 in "Part Two:.Tournament Theory."

They're Broke
— They're Done

(First, let me remind you that we are assuming either a no rebuy tournament or a tournament where the option to rebuy has expired. Proper strategy when the rebuy option is on may be rather different from what we will discuss below.)

The fact is that almost everyone who plays a tournament is playing more cautiously than usual because, unlike a side game, they cannot continue to play if they lose all their chips. The only exceptions are those who have already garnered quite a few chips, or players who are not taking the tournament that seriously. Thus, it is quite common to see a player who is notorious for his looseness in normal games playing significantly tighter when he has a small or moderate stack in a poker tournament. Ironically, as mentioned in the previous chapter, these players are probably making a mistake. Only the very best players[6] should be avoiding slightly positive gambles to allow their bigger edges time to accumulate. The typical tournament player should not ever turn down any situation with the smallest of edges.[7] You could even argue that he should gamble in situations where he has slightly the worst of it. But that is not the way the vast majority of mediocre tournament players operate. Perhaps it is because they want to experience as much time in the tournament as possible. But whatever the reason, the fact is that your opponents will, in

---

[6] Or, specifically in no-limit tournaments, players who play short and moderate stacks better than large stacks.

[7] Since you're reading (and studying?) this book, I'm assuming you're not a typical tournament player.

general, play quite a bit tighter in the tournament than they play in side games.

In my introduction I said that if you are an excellent player, and you simply play your normal game, you will show a long run profit playing tournaments.[8] Strictly speaking, that statement is true, but only because it is assumed that your normal excellent game includes adjusting for your opponents' surprising tightness. In other words, I am assuming that as a great player you notice how tightly they are playing, and you play accordingly. If instead you played your normal game without adjusting to that tightness in your opponents, you would not beat tournaments.

The fact is that the single biggest change between proper side game strategy and proper tournament strategy arises from the fact that your opponents typically play much differently when in tournaments than in side games. The most successful tournament players use this fact to their utmost advantage. In a nutshell, what they do is aggressively go after small pots and quickly back off at the first sign of strength from their opponents.

Many tournament experts cannot beat tough side games because they don't know how to play multiway pots, and don't know how to play against players who are willing to gamble it up. But these situations are rare in tournaments. A large part of their edge simply comes from understanding something I call the "Gap Concept."

---

[8] A smaller profit, of course, than if you implement the ideas in this book.

The Gap Concept

The last two chapters would seem to pull you in two different directions as far as your general strategy in a tournament. "You're Broke — You're Done" would tend to indicate that you should play tighter than normal. "They're Broke — They're Done" would tend to indicate you should play looser than normal. Is there a way to reconcile these two apparently contradictory forces?

There is a very important general principle understood by all good poker players. That is, you need a better hand to play against someone who has already opened the betting than you would need to open yourself. For instance, in jacks-or-better draw poker you might open with a pair of queens, but you would never call someone who has already opened when you hold those same two queens. In limit hold 'em, you would most certainly raise in middle position with

especially if no one else was in yet, but you would rarely play against an early position raiser with that same hand.

The difference between the hand you need to call an opener with, and that with which you would open yourself, I call the "Gap." How wide that Gap is depends on how tight your opponents play. If your opponents are quite loose, there may be no gap at all. Playing lowball draw in middle position, you can open with:

30

a one card draw to a smooth eight. But you would normally call an opener only with a one-card draw to a smooth seven. If however, the opener is extremely loose, you can call him with that eight draw. Likewise, you could play against a very loose early position hold 'em raiser with the same minimum hands that you yourself would open raise with.

So, it should be obvious that the Gap can range from non-existent to quite high. And, in a tournament, this Gap is often extremely high. In other words, in a tournament it is often right to open raise with hands far inferior to those with which you would need to call someone else who open raised.

If you think about it, you should see that this strategy coincides perfectly with the principles of the previous two chapters. You avoid confrontations with those who have already shown strength, and you take advantage of those who are trying to preserve their chips. Here are a couple of examples:

1. In limit hold 'em, if three people fold, you should probably raise with:

or

On the other hand, in this same position, if the under-the-gun player has raised, you should often consider folding a hand as good as

or

2. In stud, if no one except the bring-in has entered the pot, you should usually raise with the highest upcard showing (not duplicated elsewhere), but if someone else raises, you should usually fold any pair lower than the denomination of the upcard that had raised, especially if your kicker is also lower. In addition, you should be less apt to play drawing hands, such as

or three straights, since your pot and implied odds would usually be less than they would be in a side game

Believe it or not, this one strategy adjustment, along with otherwise good play, accounts for about half of the extra success top tournament players have compared to good side game players who don't increase their "Gap."

Of course, there are exceptions to the Gap Concept. For one, you must be aware of what kind of players are behind you and what kind of situations they are in. If the players behind you have either a very small or very large stack, loosening up on your normal opening requirements may be unwise. Players with small stacks are often ready to give up, and will therefore be quite apt to call you. Players with large stacks are no longer worried about going broke, so they too are probably playing less tightly than they were earlier.

The exception to the other side of the Gap Concept (where someone else has opened) will occur if the raiser in front of you has a lot of chips, or if he is not worried about going broke, *or* if he himself is aware of the Gap Concept. Against players like that, you are giving up too much if you significantly tighten up compared to your normal playing strategy. Another exception is when you are playing no-limit and the raiser plays worse than you.

As important as the Gap Concept is anytime in a tournament, it becomes more important still with the Gap usually widening even more during the last stages of the tourney. The reason is related to the way prizes are paid. This will be explored in more detail in the chapter called "Prize Structure Implications" starting on page 38 in "Part Two: Tournament Theory.".

I want to finish this chapter with one final thought. Since the first edition of this book appeared in 2002 there has been some confusion over the "Gap Concept." First off, it's not something I invented or claimed to have invented. The gap is something that all good poker players, at least intuitively, have known for a very long time.

But what the Gap Concept does do, as discussed above, is to allow you to adjust to how many of your opponents will play, especially when compared to a side game. It rationalizes why you should play looser in some spots, and tighter in others. It also is one of the main forces which the top tournament players use to outplay their weaker opponents.

Getting Started

Afterthought

Mathematical expectation covers any gamble. Generally speaking, if you have the best of it, you want to bet (or raise). But there is an important exception. This occurs when your bankroll is not unquestionably large enough to withstand the natural fluctuations of the game at hand. When that happens, you should pass on some bets.

This is exactly what happens in tournament poker. Your bankroll, since it is limited to what you can buy-in for, becomes top priority. Thus, you need to understand the implications of "You're Broke — You're Done" and "They're Broke — They're Done," and how all of this affects "The Gap Concept." Ignoring this area will keep your long term results only marginally profitable at best, even if you are an otherwise excellent player.

Of course, there is more to tournament strategy than just understanding how the potential to go broke can, and should, affect play. These other important factors will be covered in the rest of this text. But the previous three chapters are extremely important, and if they were not totally clear, I suggest that you read them again, and again, until they are.

Part Two
Tournament Theory

Tournament Theory

Introduction

Even though this section of the book is called "Tournament Theory" we are already well into that subject. But there is more to tournaments than just the Gap Concept and the avoidance of going broke. Those ideas are extremely important, but they are not the only forces that impact what your proper strategy should be and how your play should sometimes stray from proper side game strategy.

So what are some of the additional aspects of a poker tournament that cause you to make strategy adjustments? They include the prize structure, how the chips change value, the impact of your table being broken up, rising stakes, different stack sizes, being all-in, getting close to the money, and final table play.

None of these factors have much impact, if any, on how you should play in a standard side game. But poker tournaments are a different story. We'll see that sometimes you should play hyper aggressively and what may look to the unknowledgeable opponent as almost "maniacal," while at other times you should play what is usually called (derogatorily) "weak-tight." In fact, both these tactics are part of an overall "tough" tournament strategy.

Prize Structure Implications

In the old days, tournaments sometimes ended with a specified number of players keeping what they had in front of them. In tournaments like these, there was little advantage to surviving with a few chips, since they had only the value of those few chips that you kept. In any case, casinos preferred offering tournaments that went down to one player, since they were more dramatic. But since they wanted to give out more than first prize, they devised a scheme where each prize was a certain percentage of the total buy-in. And the prize you won depended solely on how many players were still playing when you were eliminated. It did not matter how much money you had remaining before that last hand (except to break ties when two or more players were eliminated on the same hand).

One result of this prize structure scheme is that you have a major interest in the outcome of hands that you don't play. With few exceptions, it is to your advantage for someone else to go broke. Thus, when a large stack is playing against a small stack, you are usually rooting for the large stack.

The above is pretty much common sense. But I want to take you through a simple mathematical example to demonstrate just how clear cut this is.

Suppose there are three people left in the tournament. They each have $1,000 in front of them. First prize is 60 percent of the total ($1,800). Second prize is 30 percent ($900). Third prize is 10 percent ($300). All three players play equally well. Therefore, on average, each player would (if this situation was repeated a large number of times) obviously go home with $1,000.

$$\$1,000 = \frac{\$3,000}{3}$$

Now, suppose you are one of these three players, and the other two move all-in against each other. When the hand is over, you will have second place locked up, and you will be facing someone who has $2,000. In such a situation, your chances of winning is one out of three, since you have a third of the chips.[9] That means that you will go home with $1,800 one-third of the time, and $900 two-thirds of the time. That's an average of $1,200.

$$\$1,200 = \left(\frac{1}{3}\right)(\$1,800) + \left(\frac{2}{3}\right)(\$900)$$

Before the hand started, your expected pay-off was $1,000. Merely *watching* the other two play against each other increased your EV by 20 percent, from $1,000 to $1,200. The other two both went down to an average of $900 each

$$\$900 = \frac{\$3,000 - \$1,200}{2}$$

This calculation is very telling. It shows how wonderful it is to sit back and let others go broke, and how bad it is to risk large sums on breakeven situations late in a tournament. In fact, even if you have a decent edge, it could be wrong to gamble. For instance,

---

[9] See the chapter entitled "Freezeout Calculations" starting on page 118 in "Part Three: Other Topics."

in the example given, suppose one of the players has a 54 percent chance of winning the heads-up confrontation. If that were so, he will come in third, and win $300 46 percent of the time; he will come in first and win $1,800 36 percent of the time (two-thirds of 54), and he will come in second and win $900 18 percent of the time. Well, that is an average of $948,

$$\$948 = (.46)(\$300) + (.36)(\$1,800) + (.18)(\$900)$$

which means that he still lost $52 by moving in as a 54 percent favorite. Clearly, this aspect of the tournament must be taken into account, especially when you are fighting for places along the lines of second, third, fourth, and fifth. (Unless, of course, your main goal is to win. If that matters more than the money, throwing away a 54 percent chance of doubling up is almost certainly wrong.)

So what does this all mean?

If you lose money by going all-in, as a 54-to-46 favorite, (and in fact you would have to be above 58.33 percent not to lose money in the specific scenario given) what is one supposed to do? If everybody simply sits back and waits for their opponents to play major pots against each other, nothing will ever happen.

The fact is, though, that you can take advantage of the paradox shown in this chapter. While it is certainly true that calling all-in hurts you if you are 54 percent, and even more so if you are 46 percent, what about if you are the one who makes the first bet? By being the "aggressor" in this situation, you find yourself more likely than usual to win small pots that you bet into (as long as your opponent is familiar with the concepts in this chapter).

For instance, suppose you bet $2,000 into a $100 pot with three of you remaining. If that is about equal to the stack of one of your opponents, he will probably fold a hand he would normally call with, so as not to increase the EV of the third player who is out of the pot. If he did call, he would hurt you even more than he would hurt himself. But unless he is the type to cut off his nose to spite his face, he won't do it. Rather, he will simply wait for those times when he can be the first one to bet, thus putting intolerable pressure on you, since you also do not want to add EV to the player sitting out.

Notice that the Gap Concept, previously discussed, becomes even stronger when the players are in the money or close to it. The Gap between opening and calling has increased further still. Against players who are aware of the disadvantage of fighting close decisions when others gain by watching, you can aggressively steal small pots, even if they suspect this is what you are doing. But remember that this play assumes not only that your opponent is aware of the concept, but also that he has a moderate amount of chips left. You are more apt to be called if his stack is small or large.

If it is the other player who raises, the calculations of this chapter showed that you need an even better hand than usual to play, even better than you would have at the beginning of the tournament. This is not as true if you know your opponent is aware of the Gap Concept, or if his small or large stack makes it likely he is gambling. But even in these cases, the nature of the prize distribution forces you to often let him succeed in his aggression when he is first. As I said, the Gap discussed earlier typically becomes very wide at the end of a tournament.

I will have more to say about strategy at the end of a tournament, later.

When They Call You

This book will not have a real lot to say about later round play. That might surprise those of you who know that I believe most of a good player's profit come in those later rounds. But again, this book is not purporting to teach you how to play winning poker. It is teaching you how to change your winning strategies when you are in a tournament.

And the fact is, most of your strategy changes come early in the hand. That's because the risk of going broke, the prize structure, and the all-in possibilities that influence how you should play in a tournament, have the greatest impact on your early round decisions.

But there is one very important exception. The Gap Concept of the previous chapter has you raising with *more* starting hands than you might normally be used to. It also assumes that they are calling your raises with *fewer* hands. Those two facts have a significant impact on your later round play, especially the very next round.

To properly explain this impact, we must separate seven-card stud from hold 'em or Omaha. More on that in a moment. For now, realize that when you take advantage of the Gap Concept, you will sometimes find yourself in a position which you have raised and have been called by a hand that you know is quite a bit better than yours. Even when you have raised with a good hand, you can be fairly sure that those who have called, have a better hand than you are used to facing in this situation. (This chapter is not addressing those times when you get reraised. When that happens your proper strategy is pretty much the same as it would be in a non-tournament.)

We can break things down into three possible situations:

1. They called you when you had a great hand.

2. They called you when you had a good hand.

3. They called you when your hand is below your usual requirements.

In all of these cases their hand can be expected to be better than normal. So how does that impact the next round?

If your hand happens to be quite good, you should be prepared to sandbag more than usual — be more likely to check raise on the next round, or possibly the round after that (either because you check called on the previous round or bet and were called).

Here's an example from seven-card stud. You raise with

and are called by

Since he is more likely than usual to have queens, you should often try for a check raise on fourth or fifth street when you catch non-threatening looking cards.

Here's an example from limit hold 'em. You raise with

The flop is

You bet (the flop) and get called. You should usually go for a check raise on fourth street.

If your hand is merely good, you should often immediately go into a check calling mode even though you would tend to be aggressive in a normal side game. You are up against a good hand, so if you check, he will probably bet your hand for you, even when it is slightly worse than yours. In some situations it might be right to throw in a raise to find out where you're at, thereby allowing you to get rid of your hand if reraised. But usually simply checking and calling is the preferred strategy.

Limit hold 'em example: You raise with

and get called. The flop is:

Proper tournament strategy is to frequently go into a defensive shell and just check and call. In a standard ring game you would be much more inclined to bet.

If your hand is worse than usual, be prepared to be done with it on the next round. Don't forget, his hand is better than usual. So unless the flop or fourth street has been kind to you, you should usually simply check and fold to a bet on the next round. This goes against normal poker strategy in which the early aggressor almost always fires at least one more "barrel" if he is called. That is usually not right in a tournament where you must take into consideration the necessity of conserving chips, the fact that you are up against a better than usual hand, and the fact that your hand is not as good as it normally would be.

There is, however, an important exception regarding hold 'em and Omaha high-low-split eight-or-better. The exception occurs when ragged small cards come in hold 'em, or big cards in Omaha high-low-split eight-or-better. If your raise is called before the flop in a hold 'em tournament, there is a good chance ragged low cards will not have hit your opponent. Thus if you happen to have one of those semi-steal hands like it is probably worth taking a shot at the pot on the flop when it comes something like

For similar reasons, you should often try to steal the pot from your opponent who called you in Omaha high-low-split eight-or-better when the flop comes two or more high cards.

In stud an exception (to giving up when caught with a weak hand) occurs when you catch scary cards on board, and your opponent doesn't. If you raise with

and get called by a queen, you should certainly bet again if your next card is the K♦. And if you are called, you should probably bet a third time if fifth street is a ten or higher (or a nine or a seven). Otherwise, you should probably check and fold if he bets.

Sometimes you can make a play the opposite of what has been described, particularly in a no-limit hold 'em tournament. If a very weak player raises, you might call (in late position) if no one else is in. On the flop, if your opponent checks and your hand is weak, a bet will often steal it.

Chips Change Value

Some of you may have heard the idea that each individual chip that you win is worth less than the previous ones. This is a true statement, especially regarding the vast majority of tournaments that pay a fixed prize structure, that depends on when you were eliminated.[10]

For example, suppose you were playing the $10,000 No-Limit Hold 'em World Championship at the World Series of Poker, and were allowed to sell your chips to an outsider who would take over your seat. How much would those chips be worth to him assuming he was a break even player who could be expected to break even in the long run. Obviously if he bought them right at the beginning, the answer would be $10,000.

But what the principle in the first sentence is illustrating, is that as your chips increase that bystander should no longer pay you their value to have a fair transaction. The easiest way to show this is to imagine that you have brought your chips all the way up to $3,000,000 (out of the approximately $5,000,000 in total buy-ins). That bystander would be quite dense to pay you even $2,000,000 for those chips, since first prize, as of this writing, is $2,000,000.[11]

(There are however some exceptions to this principle. To give another extreme example, suppose you have brought your $10,000 up to $230,000, and there are only three players left. Since third

---

[10] This was first shown by Mason Malmuth in his book *Gambling Theory and Other Topics.*

[11] Because of the poker boom, these numbers have gone way up. In 2006, first place paid $12,000,000. But the principle remains the same.

prize is in the neighborhood of $700,000, you would be the idiot if *you* sold them for face value.)

There is another point. The above example assumes that you are a typical player. Suppose that you are one of the best players in the tournament. Or alternatively, suppose the bystander is. It might be worth it for him to buy your original $10,000 in chips for $30,000 because of his great skill. And if you increased your $10,000 to $21,000, it might be worth it for him to pay $50,000 for that larger stack.

In other words, the extra $11,000 you won, would allow you to charge him $20,000 more. On the other hand, in this second example, even though your $11,000 win made you $20,000, it did not violate the principle that extra chips won had less value, because your first $10,000 was worth $30,000 (to the bystander anyway), while the second $11,000 was worth less than that.

The bottom line is that, with a few exceptions, what you gain by winning a chip is not quite as much as what you lose when you lose a chip. We have already covered this idea with different words, and have described the strategy changes that should be employed to take advantage of this concept. I merely wanted to address that often repeated principle and show you where it comes from.

Note: This new edition has a second chapter, "Chips Changing Value in Tournaments Revisited" starting on page 113 in "Part Three: Other Topics," elaborating further on this subject.

Keeping the Pot Small

There are two more reasons I recommend you do not push small edges early in the hand unless you have a chance to steal the pot. It is not just that you reduce your risk by saving a bet, it is also that an extra raise on your part changes the nature of the whole hand from that point forward.

An extra raise by you makes the pot bigger, which in turn forces everyone to stay in longer. You might have to take cards off that you would not have had if the pot had been smaller. This increases your volatility. Worse yet, the bigger pots mean that your opponent will chase more often when you have the best hand. And that of course might result in his winning a pot that you would have otherwise won. If you are one of the best players in the game, and are trying to maximize your tournament result, this extra volatility is something to avoid.

In no-limit hold 'em this idea does not hold as long as everyone has plenty of chips. That's because your future bets can be sized to control the odds you are offering your opponent. However, in games like limit hold 'em or seven-card stud, this is certainly not the case where raises on the early street will have the effect of offering your opponent better odds on the later streets.

Another reason to keep the pot small, true both in tournaments and non-tournaments, is that opponents' hands become easier to read. Since they are getting lower odds, the fact that they are staying in ought to allow you to narrow down their possible holdings more than you could if the pot was big. Of course, the same could be said for their being able to read your hand more easily. But as one of the best players, we should assume that the reading hands advantage helps you more than it does them.

The First Level

In many tournaments the first level is at very small stakes compared to the buy-in. This is especially true in the larger tournaments where players may have come a long distance to play. Tournament organizers like to make sure that those players have almost no chance of busting out early, so at the very least they get a few hours of play for their money. Since your results in the first level of tournaments like these are almost inconsequential to your eventual chances of winning, you may want to consider playing much looser than you will in succeeding levels.[12] This is especially true if you don't expect your table to be broken up for awhile.

Of course, in no-limit tournaments players can and do bust out at anytime, including right at the beginning of play. But even here, because of the large chip stacks relative to the blinds, the likelihood that someone goes out on a bluff or a good second-best hand is reduced.

The reason, of course, is that you are trying to create an impression you can take advantage of when the stakes rise. I have already mentioned that in limit tournaments your early tight, timid play will allow you to steal pots later on as the stakes go up. On the other hand, timid play might cost you a bit of money. One way to alleviate that problem is by playing rather loose during the first level only. Then, during the second and third level you revert to tighter play, while from the fourth level on you would typically continue to play tight, but make more frequent aggressive stabs at stealable pots.

---

[12] The main exception is discussed in the new "Part Five: Additional No-Limit Hold 'em Concepts" starting on page 213. It occurs when you are more adept with shorter stack play. If so you should definitely not splash around in no-limit hold 'em when your stack is large.

Hourly Rate Considerations

Suppose you were playing a $1,000 freezeout heads-up match against a truly awful player. Because he plays so terribly, you can almost guarantee yourself a win by grinding him down, and taking no chances. You might be able to steal lots of antes, get him to call you on the end when he has no chance, and do other things to almost ensure a win. Because of that, you choose to stay away from big pots where you are only a small favorite. For instance, you wouldn't put in a lot of money on fourth street when playing stud, even if your first four cards were a four-card straight flush.

By playing this way, you estimate that you have a 90 percent chance of winning the freezeout. That means that this freezeout is worth $800 to you in expected value.

$$\$800 = (.90)(\$1,000) - (.10)(\$1,000)$$

(If you played it 10 times, you expect to be ahead $8,000.) If the average number of hours this freezeout took was five, your expected hourly rate would be $160 per hour.

$$\$160 = \frac{\$800}{5}$$

What if you chose to gamble it up with him, pushing small edges and generally playing bigger pots? Suppose you estimated that this strategy reduced your chances of winning the freezeout to 75 percent? But suppose that playing this way meant the typical freezeout only took two hours, as opposed to five? Your expected earn per freezeout has gone down to $500.

$$\$500 = (.75)(\$1,000) - (.25)(\$1,000)$$

52

but your hourly rate has increased to $250.

$$\$250 = \frac{\$500}{2}$$

So which way should you play?

There is no definitive answer. It depends on a few different things, the most important of which is what are those saved hours worth to you? If you would have spent them idly, you probably would prefer to make more money at a lower hourly rate. Most people, if offered the opportunity to make $800 in five hours, or $500 in two hours, would choose the former, as long as the job was not too taxing. Unless you are quite wealthy it would be hard to justify giving up $300 merely to gain three hours of leisure.

On the other hand, if you had an opportunity to make money during those three hours, the situation is different. For instance, if someone was willing to pay you $150 an hour to babysit during those three hours, you should, in theory, play the shorter freezeout, earn your $500 in expected value, and then pick up another $450 from your babysitting job. That $950 is better than the $800 you would theoretically earn if you played the long, drawn out way.

Another time that you would opt to play the shorter, though less profitable freezeout, would be when you knew that you could play more than one freezeout with this guy. If he is willing to play you 10 hours a day, playing as many $1,000 freezeouts as he can fit in, you would make a lot more EV wise ($2,500 versus $1,600) by opting to gamble. (You also would be more likely to keep him coming back, since he would quit sooner if you were winning 90 percent of the matches.)

There is, however, one other possible reason to play the more conservative style: Namely, your bank roll. If you only have a few thousand dollars to your name, winning the freezeout is too important to take chances, and this is the situation for most people who play tournaments. Unless there is a juicy side game, or perhaps a juicy evening satellite tournament that you know you could get into if you go broke early in the tournament, there is little reason to be concerned about your hourly rate when playing tournaments.

If George makes $100,000 a year in 200 tournaments where he is actually sitting at the table 1,000 hours, he has made $100 an hour. If Jane, playing the same 200 tournaments, has sat at the table 1,500 hours, and made $120,000, she has earned only $80 an hour. But most would prefer Jane's results over George's. The strategies recommended in this book assume that you would too. And it is yet another reason why avoiding slightly positive EV situations (that can get you broke) are usually the right thing to do.

Limping

When discussing the Gap Concept, we were assuming that the opener, whether it be you or someone else, brought it in for a raise. In that case we learned that good tournament strategy usually means a large gap between what you would raise with, and what you would call (or reraise) with. But what about merely calling to open? Should you ever do that? And what if they merely call? Poker players have a name for this type of opening. They call it "limping."

In general, you should rarely limp in a limit hold 'em tournament. There is simply too great a chance that you will steal the blinds with a raise. You give up that chance when you limp. Those hands that you might limp in with in a ring game hoping to get multiway action now do better with a raise, if they are played at all, because multi-player pots are much rarer in tournaments. Thus, hands like

or

under-the-gun, if played at all, should usually be brought in with a raise.

Remember, however, we are speaking of limit rather than no-limit. When all your chips can be in play at anytime, and the stacks are still deep relative to the blinds, limping or small raises can clearly be correct if they have the potential of allowing you to make a big hand that might trap your opponent for a lot of chips.

On the other hand, once the stakes have increased to the point where many of the stacks are in jeopardy, you should revert to the more standard raise if first in strategy. Put another way, the Gap Concept doesn't apply (pre-flop) in the early rounds of a no-limit hold 'em tournament where the stack size is great compared to the blinds.

It's also a little different for Omaha high-low-split eight-or-better, or seven-card stud. Since it is rare to steal the blinds in Omaha high-low-split eight-or-better, even in a tournament, you may choose to limp with some hands in early position, just as you would in a side game. I won't go into which hands those are because this is not a book on poker strategy. For those who are interested in Omaha high-low-split eight-or-better, I suggest *High-Low-Split Poker for Advanced Players* by Ray Zee.

Playing seven-card stud tournaments, you will limp fairly often, just as you would in a side game. The difference between seven-card stud and hold 'em is that one of your cards is showing. Because of that, you cannot as easily represent a powerful hand when your upcard is small, and thus have little chance of an ante steal in those situations. The most obvious example of when you should probably limp is when you have a live three flush with a small card showing such as

If, however, your three flush was with a high upcard such as

and no one else is yet in, you revert back to the Gap Concept, and would raise with this hand more than you would in a side game, knowing that the chances of winning right there have increased. (Notice that the two sample hands above each contain the same three cards. But the first one has the 4♥ up, and the second one has the J♥ in the door.)

Getting back to mainly hold 'em, what if someone limps in front of you? Because it is a tournament, even limpers will tend to be tighter than they would be in side games. Therefore, you should also be more selective. If your hand is merely good, you should be more apt to simply limp behind them rather than raise. In fact, you would generally need a better hand to limp behind a limper than you would need to raise with if no one was yet in. To raise that limper, you need a better hand yet.

In a hold 'em tournament, if a good player limped in first position, and I was in middle position, would probably hit the muck (but be played if the hand was suited). However, I would probably call with

In stud, if a small card limped in I would not usually raise without a big pair even though in a side game I would often raise with a hand like

No-limit hold 'em is different. The best players should be doing a lot of limping, even with mediocre hands. As previously mentioned, the Gap Concept doesn't apply (pre-flop) in the early rounds where the stack size is great compared to the blinds.

Actually, the Gap Concept only kicks in when the stack sizes are smaller compared to the antes and the blinds. On the later rounds you can make a lot of plays at the pot without very much, but quickly give up with pretty good hands if someone else is betting. Before the flop, however, implied odds and superior skill allow you to limp with lots of hands with decent prospects, whether or not players have limped in front of you. (For more on this I recommend my book. co-written with Ed Miller, *No-Limit Hold 'em: Theory and Practice*.)

When Will
Your Table Break Up?

One difference between a tournament and a side game is that after a while, due to the combining of tables as people go broke, you will often find yourself against completely different opponents.[13] This has implications to your strategy, especially if you have some idea when your table will break up. (Many tournaments have a preordained set order for breaking tables. Sometimes this order is announced to everyone, and sometimes it isn't. If nothing has been announced, you should try to find out for yourself by asking a tournament director what the plans are regarding the future breaking up of your table.)

If it looks like your table will break up soon, that has two possible effects on your strategy. The obvious one is that you make no "advertising" plays, since you will probably not have time to reap the benefits. Don't make an ill conceived bluff in hopes of eliciting calls later on. Don't play extra timidly to try and set up a bluff in the future. The people you are trying to set up won't be in your game in a few minutes.

The other time you might change your strategy if your table is scheduled to break up soon is when you are playing against much tougher opponents than the average player in the rest of the room. When you are at a table like that, it would be a shame to go broke, or near broke when a much easier table is soon coming along. This is yet another example of a tournament situation

---

[13] In major tournaments there is sometimes a complete redraw for seats. This usually occurs when tournaments extend to a second day. All remaining players come back that next day to new seats. There is also frequently a redraw when the tournament reaches the final two or three tables.

where you might choose to pass up a small edge to increase the chances of finding a larger edge in the future. This principle is especially true if you are playing no-limit or pot-limit. If your tough table will be soon broken up, stay away from close gambles.

(When I say "soon" broken up, I would typically mean within an hour or two. But it depends on your stack and how fast the stakes are going up. You may not have time to wait that long, and will have to gamble with your chips if you do. On the other hand, sometimes you can wait even longer. The first day of the $10,000 No-Limit Hold 'em World Championship at the World Series of Poker, the blinds start out so small and move up so slowly that few tables are broken up until a fair number of hours have passed. The second day, however, everyone redraws for seats. In this tournament, when my initial table is extra tough, I am willing to wait many hours and be content to bring my $10,000 buy-in up to $15,000 or $20,000, rather than risk going broke and missing my chance to play against worse players the next day.)

If it is obvious that you will have to play at a table for a long time, your strategy switches from the above. Setting up plays for the future are even more important to do than in regular side games. Your opponents will be exactly the same, and the play you set up will be most likely at bigger stakes than the original play you used to start the process. If you find yourself at a tough table that will not break up, you have to make the best of it. You can't play extra tightly in the hopes of conserving your chips for a different table. You must simply accept that you are in trouble if you get worse than average cards, and therefore, play in such a way that will win you some chips if you do get lucky.

Adjusting Strategy Because the Stakes Rise

Is there any reason to adjust strategy because the stakes rise every hour or so? There may very well be, but not in the way you may think. I have often heard it said that if your stack is short, you must take chances *now* because you will not have enough chips to play with once the stakes go up. That is totally wrong. In fact, if anything, the reverse is true.

One time this is obvious is near the end of the tournament where your short stack is a bit smaller than some opponents. At the present stakes your opponent has more than enough chips to avoid going broke on one hand. But at the next level, he doesn't. If the stakes will soon rise, you should avoid taking risks in marginal situations at the lower limit, since there is a better chance you will be able to sneak into a higher money position at the higher stakes where the stacks that are slightly ahead of you are apt to bust out. Put another way, once the stakes are increased, those opponents who have a small chip lead over you have less of an edge since all of you are now in a position of risking going broke if you play a hand to the river. So that is a reason you would actually play a little tighter until the stakes are raised, to try to get into that position.

Here's an example. Suppose you are playing limit hold 'em and have reached the money. The stakes are now $100-$200. If there is betting on every round it can cost you at least $600 (in tournament chips). ($100 before the flop, $100 on the flop, $200 on the turn, and $200 on the river.) So, if you have less than that and one of your opponents has a little more, perhaps $800, you may want to play a little tighter than normal if the stakes will soon be raised.

Let's say you do this, the stakes are doubled, and your chip positions haven't changed. Now you need at least $1,200 to play a hand to the river. But notice that the advantage the $800 chip holder has over you has been reduced for now. Unlike before, he cannot complete a hand and still have chips left if there has been betting all the way through.

Another reason to consider playing a bit tighter before the stakes rise has to do with one of your superior skills. This might sound strange, because in general skillful players lose some of their advantage as their chips go down. But this can reverse when that player's stack is very small. The reason is that superior players are well versed in the value of various hands in all-in situations. Most tournament players, however, are rather inept at knowing what to do when they or their opponent might be going all-in early in the hand. So if you happen to have a stack that is a little bit bigger than what would be required to move in early, you may be better off waiting to the next raise in stakes, so that the same size stack becomes an all-in stack.[14]

The biggest reason, however, to change your strategy because of subsequent increases in stakes, are that the payoffs from creating an impression early are greater than they would be in a normal game. This can work in two different ways. You could play somewhat aggressively, or even wildly early on, in the hopes that it is noticed, and that this results in getting calls down the road that you otherwise might not have gotten when you have a big hand. That strategy pays off more in tournaments than it does in a normal game because those calls will be at bigger stakes.

The alternate strategy would be to play very tightly, and even timidly early on, in order to set up a bluff down the road. Again, this works better in a tournament than in a normal game because the pot you steal will be bigger given the raised stakes, in

---

[14] See the chapter entitled "All-in Strategy" starting on page 71 in this section for more discussion.

comparison to the loss of equity that you sustain by playing less than optimally at the smaller stakes.

So which of these two alternate strategies should you use? Obviously you usually can't use both in the same tournament. As a general rule, the answer would be that you should use the first strategy in no-limit or pot-limit tournaments, and the second strategy in limit tournaments. This is pretty much common sense, although I don't think it is a hard and fast rule. It especially may be true that the second strategy, of playing timidly at first to set up bluffs later, might be the preferred one even in no-limit or pot-limit tournaments.

You should also keep in mind that you might not be able to choose your strategy. The cards might dictate it. If for instance you have been dealt garbage the first hour, your opponents will assume you are tighter than you really are. This is the image you are stuck with. So even if you have originally planned the opposite game plan, you must now abandon it.

Of course, the above two strategies should not be used if you believe your table will be breaking up soon. (See the chapter entitled "When Will Your Table Break Up?" starting on page 59 in this section.)

Noticing the Short Stacks

The idea that you should alter your play in the tournament depending on how many chips your opponents have in front of them is probably a bit over-rated. Some tournament players make rather drastic adjustments depending on their stack compared to others. They go too far with this idea, especially in the early stages. That being said, there are in fact some adjustments that should be made.

Even putting aside strategy for the last table, it is important to pay attention to who is on a short stack. Typically, players with much less than the average amount of chips in front of them are ready to give up — hopefully you don't fall in that category. Because of this tendency, it is often unwise to make your usual semi-bluff thrust at a small pot. That play works well when players are anxious to conserve their chips. Small stacks, early in a tournament, are not thinking this way, and will be much more likely to call. (The same is almost as true for most players with large stacks. So you stay away from your normally aggressive opening style when your opponents are not mainly moderate stacks.)

Another reason to notice whether you might be up against a short stack is so that you can adjust your hand selection towards starting hands that do well "hot and cold."[15] This concept applies mainly to hold 'em, especially no-limit hold 'em, where putting your opponent all-in before the flop means the value of hands are shifted. For example,

---

[15] Hot and cold means that you are dealing out all the cards with no betting.

is normally much better than

but not if you are running the cards out against the kinds of hands (such as king-ten or king-nine) that a desperate short stack might call you with.

There is a situation where some players pay too much attention to short stacks, in spite of what you may have heard. Many so called experts advocate going much too far out of your way to eliminate players. For instance, in a multiway pot with one person all-in, they suggest "checking it down" with your other opponents who still have money, unless your hand is far superior. The idea is that by playing this way you will have increased the chances of busting the short stack because you don't drive out others. They also advocate getting all-in against a short stack, rather than leaving him with a few chips, even with hands that might not seem worth it. The idea again being that by playing this way you will guarantee his elimination when you do win the pot.

Both of these ideas are usually wrong. The only time they have some merit is at the very end of the tournament. And even then, only when you have a moderately small stack yourself. In those cases, his elimination can add quite a bit to your EV, which might indicate that you play less than what would normally be optimal, in order to increase the chances of that elimination. Aside from that one exception, however, you should not make sub-optimal plays simply because it might help eliminate that short stack. (Be glad others are doing that though.) You yourself adjust to short stacks only because you can assume they are getting desperate, and because hands that you play against them will not involve a bet on every round.

Noticing the Large Stacks

It is also important to notice those players who have large stacks. Most players in this situation have lost their fear of going broke, and are more likely both to call you with mediocre holdings, or initiate the betting with such holdings. In other words, they tend to play looser than the moderate stacks. The Gap, discussed earlier, narrows against them. You need to loosen up slightly when they open the pot, and tighten up slightly when they are behind you and you are considering opening.

This advice, of course, is a generalization. There are some players who remain quite cautious, even with a large stack. (Likewise, for some players with a short stack.) You should definitely keep your eyes out for these players who don't fit the norm, and adjust accordingly.

It's also important to realize that some players with a large stack are a little more prone to play their hands in a tricky manner. With a small stack, they will want to bet to win the pot as fast as possible to assure that they have enough chips to continue on in the tournament. But with a large stack, their view is that all options are available to them. This is especially dangerous when the tournament is no-limit hold 'em. So against a player like this, you'll need to be a little more cautious than normal.

When the Blinds are Coming Up

Suppose there is only one hand to go before your blind and you have only enough chips to put in that blind when it comes to you. There are many people who say that you should play this first hand as long as it is better then your average hand. This, in spite of the fact that it may be much worse than the hand you would normally need to play in this position. Their reasoning is that you will be forced to play an average hand (on average) your next hand, (when you are in the blind), so anything better than that would be preferable to play now.

Others reject that concept and suggest you do not alter your strategy simply because you will soon be forced to go all-in or near all-in on your blind. So who's right?

The answer is neither one. It turns out that in situations like this you should play hands worse than normal, but not merely better than average. It is somewhere in between.

Remember earlier we showed mathematically that if tomorrow you have an opportunity to make a great bet for a certain fixed amount of money, you should pass up merely good bets today if losing them will keep you from making that great bet tomorrow. With similar math we can show that the converse is also true. If you are forced to make a terrible bet tomorrow, it strangely enough, becomes right to make a merely bad bet today, if losing that bet allows you to skip tomorrow's bet. This is true, even if losing that first bet means you are broke.

For instance, if tomorrow you were forced to make an even money bet of $100, on a 20 percent shot, you should make an earlier $100 bet on as little as a 28.57 percent shot, if losing that bet means you don't bet tomorrow. Notice, however, you should not bet if you are below 28.57 percent. It is not correct to take a bad bet now to avoid an even worse bet later, if today's bet is almost as bad.

These mathematical results can be applied to the tournament situation where you are about to go close to all-in on your big blind (or in stud where you are down to your very last few antes). If you have one hand left, you need a hand that is somewhat better than your average hand to play. It cannot merely be slightly better.

If there is more than one hand to go before you are forced to put in the blind, the degree you loosen up compared to how you would play if you could quit without taking your blind, would be less. Once you get to the point where you can still wait four or five hands, there should be almost no change in your strategy as compared to normal (unless there is a significant ante). Notice, however, that when I refer to your normal strategy, I am not speaking of your strategy with lots of chips. Rather, I am speaking of normal all-in strategy (where you are not forced to play your upcoming blind short-stacked).

To show what I mean by this let's take the hand:

under-the-gun. There are many games where, with lots of chips in front of you, it is correct to limp. On the other hand, if you only have the amount of the big blind, you should fold if you were planning to quit after this hand. However, if instead, you are required to play the big blind if you fold (as you would be in a tournament) you should again call with this hand.

Note: The above concepts apply only to limit tournaments with no ante. The only time they would apply to no-limit tournaments would be if there is no ante and your stack is so tiny that a move in will scare almost no one out.

The reason why an ante changes things relates to the fact that you won't win as much on average if you win the next pot rather than this one. (A fact missed in the first edition.)

All-In Strategy

One of the major differences between regular poker games and tournament poker is that in the tournaments a player is often all-in. The correct strategy involving all-in decisions is usually the same for both side games and tournaments. However, these situations come up so infrequently in a side game that the knowledge concerning how to play them is not needed to be a successful side game player. That is not the case in tournaments.

Notice that you need to understand all-in concepts, not only because you will often be a short stack, but also because you will often be *against* a short stack. Either way there will be no further betting on later rounds, so you must know which hands to choose to play in these situations.

Before going into some specifics, I want to mention an important point regarding being all-in. That point is that it is actually to your advantage to be out of chips, especially if it is early in a hand. This might seem intuitively wrong, particularly if you are a very good player, because your weapons (namely your chips) have been taken away from you. All you can do is helplessly watch the cards come off and hope your hand wins. However, in spite of the fact that being all-in keeps you from using your skill, this is more than made up for, on average, by the fact that you are guaranteed to see the last card.

To give an extreme example, suppose you are playing seven-card stud and are all-in for the ante. If you are playing in an eight handed game you would win one out of eight pots if everyone went to the river. But since many of the players are folding, you will sometimes win pots that otherwise would have been won by one of those players who threw their hand away. Depending on how players play, you might win one in five of those pots you were all-in. Thus you would be getting 7-to-1 odds on a 4-to-1

71

shot. If you were playing $30-$60 with a $5 ante, your expected profit would be $3.00.

$$\$3 = \left(\frac{1}{5}\right)(7)(\$5) - \left(\frac{4}{5}\right)(\$5)$$

If you could do this every hand, you would make about $100 an hour in a brick and mortar casino, which is much more than even great players make with lots of chips in front of them.

Because being all-in is so advantageous, the advice you often hear to start playing poor hands when your stack is short, since you no longer have time to wait for a good hand, is for the most part wrong (except in extreme situations discussed in the previous chapter). There is no reason to play much weaker hands to avoid going all-in soon thereafter. Even if you throw all your hands away until that one last hand, where you are forced all-in, it is not so terrible. To give up sooner than that and play a very bad hand is a big mistake.

The subject of all-in play is quite complex, especially when more than two people are involved. Even if only heads-up situations are considered, there are so many different possibilities that could be mathematically analyzed as to allow a whole book to be written about it. In this chapter I will merely outline some basic situations and what needs to be considered in those situations.

Basically there are four heads-up situations that could result in an all-in pot:

1. You are the short stack and the aggressor.
2. You are the short stack and the defender.
3. You are the larger stack and the aggressor. And,
4. You are the larger stack and the defender.

Let us examine these one by one. (These situations are more clear cut in hold 'em than in seven-card stud or Omaha high-low-split eight-or-better, so I will use hold 'em for my examples. Those who are playing other games will have to extrapolate.)

Suppose you are playing limit hold 'em and are in the big blind, and all you have left is just enough to call a raise. All fold to the small blind, who raises without looking at his cards. You have

Should you call?

What we have here is a pure math problem. In fact, almost all of these all-in situations are pure math problems. That should be obvious since there is no further betting and no further skill. Anyway, in this particular case the answer is definitely yes. Why? Because a trey-deuce has (coincidentally) a 32 percent chance of beating two random cards, and you are getting 3-to-1 on this call.[16]

(The reason I know that trey-deuce has a 32 percent chance is because I own a computer program that will let you punch in one hand against another or one specified hand against one random hand. Serious tournament players must purchase one of these programs. They are also now available on the Internet at no cost)

The example I gave was rather simple. We knew his hand was random because he never looked at his cards, and you had exactly enough money to call his raise. I can tell you right now that in this specific situation, (i.e. you are in the big blind) where a player is either raising in the dark or is in a strategic situation

---

[16] Trey-deuce is the worst possible hand played against two random cards "hot and cold," i.e. no betting.

where he will raise with just about anything, you must call no matter what you have. (There is one possible exception. If you throw your hand away here and then throw the next hand away also, you will have half a big blind in front of you that could conceivably be enough to move you up in the standings. Thus, if one or more players besides you have tiny stacks and figure to go broke when the blind comes to them, you would fold many hands, so you could squeak into a higher money position.) You are getting at least 3-to-1 odds and no two cards are that much of an underdog to a random or near random hand.

It gets a lot more ticklish, however, if

1. You have more than enough to call.

2. It is a no-limit hand where his raise gives you less than 3-to-1 odds to call. Or,

3. The hand you are facing is to varying degrees better than random.

Suppose the big blind was $100 (in tournament chips), the small blind was $50, you had another $200 in chips, and the small blind again raised in the dark. Since we can assume that the small blind will probably bet any flop and that you are often forced to call (getting 5-to-1 odds at this point), the true or effective odds you are getting before the flop are not 300-to-100 but are in fact 400-to-200. This makes calls with your absolute worst hands more borderline.

If you are playing no-limit, the size of your opponent's raise now becomes very relevant. Thus, even if you think he will raise with anything, you should still throw away your worst hands when his raise will put you all-in and give you odds of 2-to-1 or worse. So if you are in a $100 blind, have $400 or more in front of you, and your opponent moves you in, you are getting $600-to-$400 odds (or 3-to-2). And even if his hand is random, you can't call unless you have something along the lines of

since this hand will win a little better than 40 percent of the time against a random holding.

Suppose you have some inkling about what type of hands your opponent will raise you with. If that is the case, you can, in theory, calculate which hands to call with based on his possible holdings and the odds you are getting. In order to do this well you have to have done some research away from the table using one of these computer programs along with some combinatorics.[17]

To give an overly simplified example, suppose you were in the big blind with $100 and held

Your opponent in the small blind attempted to move you in with a $600 bet (thus giving you 7-to-5 odds), and you put your opponent on aces, kings, or ace-king (far tighter than most opponents would play). Two jacks is in big trouble against two out of three of those hands. To make the call right, the jacks must win

---

[17] This new edition now contains a chart in "Two Wonderful Charts" starting on page 252 in "Part Five: Additional No-Limit Hold 'em Concepts" that pretty much does this for you.

more than 41 percent of the time. But it is too simplistic to say that the jacks are in trouble two out of three times and you should fold. That is because the aces and kings are dealt less often than ace-king. On the other hand, the aces and kings are bigger favorites over jacks than jacks are over ace-king.

To get the answer you must do some calculating. First you must realize that a pair of aces can be dealt in six different ways. Ditto for the kings. Ace-king, on the other hand, can be dealt in 16 different ways. Meanwhile, when the jacks are facing one of the 12 combinations of aces or kings, they will win only about 2 of those 12 times. Against the ace-king, they will win about 9 of the 16 times. Altogether, therefore, they will win 11 out of 28 times.

$$11 = 2 + 9$$

$$28 = 12 + 16$$

That is 39.3 percent or just a tad short of the required 41.67 percent.

$$39.3 = (100)\left(\frac{11}{28}\right)$$

Thus, the proper play (given these extreme assumptions) is to fold. Notice, however, that a slightly smaller raise or the inclusion of ace-queen as a possible opposing hand would turn that fold into a call. As you can see, this type of calculation becomes, at best, only an estimate in the majority of situations. (By the way, if you do try to do this, you must take into account your own cards. So in the example given, if ace-jack was yet another hand that he might have, you need to realize that can only be dealt 8 ways rather than 16 because of the two jacks in your hand.)

To summarize the above, and how you could do it yourself with the aid of a computer, what you do is this: Enter your hand into the computer and run it against the possible hands that you think he could have. Let's say there were four different such hands. You will get 4 different percentages as to your chances of winning. But you cannot simply average them. That is because some of his hands will be dealt more often than others. You need to know how to count the number of combinations of the various hands he could have, including making the adjustment, when necessary, for the cards in your own hand. Armed with this information, you now take a *weighted* average of the four numbers the computer spit out, and compare that to the odds you are getting. How to calculate card combinations and take weighted averages is addressed in any good statistics or gambling book. (And again, there is now a chart in the chapter "Two Wonderful Charts" starting on page 252 in "Part Five: Additional No-Limit Hold 'em Concepts.")

As difficult as these calculations are, they become even more difficult when you, as the short stack, are considering a raise yourself. This is different from when you are considering calling because you usually have a chance of winning the pot with your raise, unchallenged. Even when you know you will get called, the calculation is a bit different, so let's do that first.

Suppose you are on the button, have $200 left, no one else is in yet, the $50 small blind is throwing his hand away out of turn (to simplify things), and you know the big blind is a good player. Because he is a good player a raise on your part will almost certainly be called as he is getting 3½- to-1 odds. Knowing he will call, how good a hand do you need to raise with? (We will assume that merely limping is not an option.) *You* are getting $250-to-$200 (or 5-to-4) odds when you raise. Remember, he will always call. That means you must win 200 out of 450 hands to have a positive EV. Therefore, you need to remember which hands have better than a 44½ percent chance of winning against a random hand, and raise with them, and throw away the others.

Let's say instead you had $500 on the button and were trying to figure out whether a raise would be profitable. This is not so easy to do. If you knew he would call you every time, it would be simple enough because getting $550-to-$500 odds, it is a simple matter to see which hands win often enough to make the play profitable. (Except for one very important thing. A profitable play is not necessarily the right play. That is because there may be another alternative which is even more profitable. In this case, where you know you will be called, it might well be better to merely limp with mediocre hands since that might show a greater long run profit than raising with them.)

But because he will fold many of his hands, you need to break things down. When he folds you win $150. Since your raise costs you $500 it would show a small profit (of $7) if it steals the pot 78 percent of the time, even if you never won those times that you were called.

$$\$7 = (.78)(\$150) - (.22)(\$500)$$

But of course you will win many of the times you are called, which means that you need not succeed in your steal anywhere near that often to make the play right. For instance, suppose you thought that he will fold half the time if you make that $500 raise. How often would you need to win those other times (when he called you) to make the overall play profitable?

I will not bore you with the algebra required to do this problem. Instead, let us throw out a number and see whether it would be enough. Suppose you stole the ante 50 percent of the time and won 30 percent of the remaining showdowns. That means that in twenty hands you would have won $150 ten times, won $550 three times, and lost $500 seven times. Your total win would be $3,150 and your total loss is $3,500.

$$\$3,150 = (10)(\$150) + (3)(\$550)$$

$$-\$3,500 = (7)(-\$500)$$

In this particular case the play would not be quite worth it. If you stole the pot slightly more often, or won the pot slightly more often when you didn't steal, this play would swing to a positive one. Again, however, remember that it doesn't mean it is the right play if an alternative play is still yet more positive.

Anyway, the break even point for the above problem, assuming he will throw his hand away half the time, is that you need to win one-third of the those times he doesn't throw his hand away. Armed with this information and a lot of patience, we can figure out about what hands are raising hands. We know about what hands he will fold, since we know he will throw half his hands away. The question now becomes, given he has a calling hand, what hands of ours will win one-third of the time, weighted average wise, against those hands?

Clearly a hand like 3♣2♥ is not one of them. It only wins 32 percent of the time against a random hand. But even hands that win 35 percent against a random hand are apt to win less than the required 33 percent against the hands that he will call with. As you can see, finding the precise answers to these questions is almost impossible. But making estimates, now that you see what is entailed, should be within your grasp.

When you have the larger stack, and a smaller stack moves in against you, it is again a math question, once you have used your judgment to determine the possible hands he will make that play with. You see what odds you are getting, you look at your hand, and you estimate his possible hands. You take the weighted average of your chances with each of those possible hands and see whether your pot odds makes the call worth it. Of course, this assumes that everyone else has already folded. If there are still players yet to act, or if other players have already called, you would need to increase the strength of your hand, perhaps significantly, before you would make this call. (Again see the new chart.)

If you are a larger stack that is contemplating putting a small stack all-in, the math is the same as it was above, where you combine your chances of stealing the pot with your chances of winning if you are called. Again this assumes that other players are out or are quite likely to be out. The difference, however, is that when you are making this play against a short stack, there is a wide range of possibilities as far as what his calling proclivities might be.

Depending on the player and the tournament situation at the time, you may be looking at a circumstance where you figure him to throw away 90 percent of his hands. If so, a moderate raise with any two cards is the right play. At other times, the short stack may be desperate, or have given up to the point where you can expect a call the majority of the time. In such cases you would need a much better hand to make this raising play.

As you can see, there is a lot to consider when hands will be played all-in. There are, however, some simple rules of thumb. In hold 'em, you should realize that certain hands go up or down in value depending on whether there will be future betting. A sometimes playable hand like

is rarely worth playing all-in, whereas a usually unplayable hand like

or

may well be worth moving in with, even though they should usually be folded if more chips are at risk later.

There is an exception with a hand like

It is when you can get 2-to-1 on your money but only be against one player.

Here's an example. Suppose an opponent raises and then a second player, who has a lot of chips, moves all-in. Furthermore, you know this player would move all-in in this spot with a wide range of hands in an attempt to pick up the pot. If you happen to have approximately the same amount of chips as the first player's raise, you may want to call. Notice that it will be very difficult for the initial raiser to call since he will think that if his other opponent doesn't have him badly beat, there is a good chance that you do. So when successful, you can get a little better than 2-to-1 on your call and your chances of winning can be significantly better than 33.3 percent.

In the case of seven-card stud, if an all-in pot seems imminent, small and medium pairs go up in value, while small

three flushes and three straights go down. So you might play a
hand like

but throw away a hand like

In Omaha high-low-split eight-or-better, a hand like

is probably worth playing all-in, even in spots where it would
normally be folded.

Just Out of the Money

The following advice assumes that there is a decent pay off for the lowest money prize. That lowest prize might be offered to the ninth place or eighteenth place in a hold 'em tournament, or eighth place or sixteenth place in a stud tournament.

Let's say everyone at the last two tables gets paid, with last place being 2 percent of the total prize pool. Suppose there are three tables left, where one or two players need to go broke before they combine into the last two tables. Should you alter your strategy because of this situation?

Well, if you have a lot of chips, you certainly should. In the next chapter, the special last two table situation is addressed where I point out how advantageous it is to be one of the chip leaders who can steal from those short stacks that are trying to sneak into the money. This really is a profitable situation. Even when you are a medium stack you can take a little advantage of it those times that the larger stacks are already out.

But what if you are one of the short stacks? Should you alter your play to try to sneak into the money? Let me stop here and make one point. Though there will be times when your overall tournament mathematical expectation can be increased by folding hands that are normally slightly profitable, you may not want to. Because by doing so, you have turned a small chance of getting a major prize into a tiny chance. This might be unpalatable to you in spite of the minor increase in EV. Given the small amount of money involved, I have no problem with anyone who chooses to make absolutely no adjustments with their short stacks rather than try to sneak into the money. In the long run, they will make slightly less than those who look only at their EV, and they will much more often get the "booby prize" of coming in one out of the money. On the other hand, they will probably slightly increase their chances to reach one of the higher prizes, which for some people is an extra reward in itself.

If, however, you are concerned about getting into the money, there are things you can do to help yourself. One of the main things is to physically get up from your table and notice how your stack compares to everyone else's, not just those at your table. You might have the lowest stack at your table, (which would mean that you may as well gamble if it was the last table), but your stack is bigger than the stack of one or two players at the other tables. Assuming we are talking about stacks that are so small that losing one hand will deplete them completely, you should stay away from all close gambles, and maybe even some not so close gambles, (e.g. calling an early raiser with

in hold 'em), if it looks like that will significantly increase your chances of getting into the money.

This situation occurs when there are some stacks smaller than yours. It also occurs when you have the smallest stack, as long as you don't think the other small stacks are going out of their way waiting for you to go broke. (If it does look like they are waiting you out, and your stack is smallest, you should play no tighter than you normally would.)

There is an exception to this that needs to be mentioned and is quite common at some of the major tournaments, especially at those with many qualifiers who have gotten into the tournament on a small investment (through a satellite) and for which the initial prizes are very small compared to the overall prize pool. Let's look at an example.

Suppose some tournament with a $10,000 buy-in has enough entries so that the overall prize pool is $5,000,000, and the initial places to receive money only get one-quarter of one percent or $12,500. For someone who might have spent less than $100 to get into the event, that $12,500 can look huge and they will often begin to play too tight.

This is what Dan Harrington in *Harrington on Hold 'em; Expert Strategy for No-Limit Tournaments; Volume II: The Endgame* refers to as an inflection point (and inflection points can occur in other spots as well). Put another way, it's a place in the tournament where the gap, for reasons that have little to do with actual strategy, can get very large. If no one is yet in, it can become correct to raise with some very questionable hands. But if someone else has already raised, especially if it appears to be a player who is very concerned about making the money, your range of playable hands should now be greatly reduced.

Just In the Money

We have just seen, especially in large tournaments, that many players will significantly tighten their play as they approach the money. That's because even though the initial payoffs are quite small relative to the total prize pool, they can still be large in absolute terms for some of the players relative to their bankrolls and/or investment into the tournament.

Once you pass this inflection point, things can and often do change dramatically. That is, once the pressure is off, some of your opponents won't care anymore since they have now accomplished what it was they came to accomplish — making the money, and now they'll play exceptionally loose trying to get lucky to put them in position to win one of the top prizes. This will be especially true if the next few places all pay the same amount.

So again we come back to our old friend, The Gap Concept. If play loosens up, the gap narrows. If play is tight, the gap widens. In this case it could narrow a lot.

(By the way, even though I'm mentioning it out of chronological order, another time when play is sometimes very loose is during the first level. That's because many participants won't perceive the initial bets as a threat to their starting stack. But once the stacks have been raised, this perception can change completely and you may wonder if you are at the same table, and once more you would adjust the gap from narrow to wide.)

A Special Last
Two Table Situation[18]

Suppose there are only two tables left, with five players at each table. If one more player goes broke, the tables are combined. The tournament pays nine places. At this point all of the short stacks are desperately trying to survive and we are at another inflection point.

The difference between tenth place and ninth place is usually pretty significant (when the last table starts with nine players), even when tenth place pays a nominal amount. With the combination of the two tables imminent (and the main money is at the final table), these short stacks will tend to throw away all but their very best hands rather than risk the booby prize (coming in 10th). Because of that, the chip leader at both tables is in a wonderful position, especially in games with blinds. When no one has yet opened, he can raise with an awful lot of hands since his chances of stealing the pot are so high. (The player with the second largest stack at each table is in a similar position if the largest stack has already folded, as long as that second largest stack is also pretty big.)

It is not uncommon for the largest stack at each of the two five handed tables to significantly increase his chip position during this time, even without ever playing a hand to the river. He merely steals the blinds hand after hand.

---

[18] Actually, this chapter could now be renamed "Last Table Out of the Money Situation." Nowadays that could happen when there are ten or more tables left.

In addition, because of this syndrome, the chip leader at each table has an opportunity to make a very unusual strategy adjustment. Suppose he is on the button with:

and the player with the shortest stack raises, almost all-in. *The two queens should consider folding!* Do you see why? The gain from playing this hand, perhaps a small bet in expected value, might not be worth the fact that if you do win the pot, the tables are combined, and you can no longer run over the game.

This of course is a rather unique situation to be in, so knowing it will not help your long term tournament results very much. I bring it up more to show how the nature of tournaments is such that they can occasionally indicate a strategy far different from what you are used to.

The Last Table

In almost all tournaments, reaching the last table means getting into the money. In some cases, significant money. Ninth place at the $10,000 No-Limit Hold 'em Championship at the World Series of Poker is over $1,000,000. And each higher place adds that much more money. Because the amount involved in moving up a place or two can be significantly more than the face value of your chips, it is almost mandatory that you take this into account if the money is important to you.

(If winning the tournament is really your only goal, more power to you. You would then not make most of the strategy adjustments that I am about to recommend when your chips are low. Just realize that you are sacrificing a lot of EV in your quest to win.)

On the other hand, many tournament players go too far trying to move up the ladder. They actually lose EV with their strategy that places too much emphasis on surviving in hopes of finishing a bit higher. The only justification for what they do would be if their bankroll was such that the extra money they often win is so important to them that it is worth *badly* hurting their chances of getting a top prize.

The strategy adjustments for the last table designed to move you up in the standings really only apply to the players with fairly short stacks. If you have a moderate stack, you should make few adjustments. For instance, if their are nine players left, and you have an average amount of chips, and are in about fifth place, you could almost certainly ante your way into getting sixth prize. But given the typically giant increase in prizes paid to the last three places, any strategy along those lines (anteing your money off) would be ridiculous. Yes, you will sometimes wind up coming in seventh or eighth by playing your normal game, but you will far more often come in the top three as well. The upside of extreme caution when you have a moderate stack is simply not worth the downside.

There is one major exception. It occurs when you are playing no-limit, and you are facing a stack that can bust you. Here you should probably not risk all your chips as a slight favorite since a loss would bring you instantly down to ninth place. This would be especially true if doubling your chips would still not make you one of the leaders.

There are some tournaments in which the lesser prizes go up very slowly. Sometimes not at all. For instance, eighth and ninth place may pay the same. In tournaments like this, there should be virtually no change in your strategy with a short stack and nine players, regardless of your chip position. Significant strategic changes might not occur until there are six or seven players left.

Each tournament is different, so you will have to use your judgment to decide to what degree you would alter your strategy due to prize structure. But the basic idea is this: *If you are in next to last place, but still quite short, you should tend to go out of your way to avoid going broke before the shorter stack does.*

(The assumption is made that if you both continue to ante or blind off your money, he would go broke first. This is almost always the case in stud [barring a lot of unlucky bring-ins]. It may not be the case in hold 'em or Omaha. He could have slightly less than you, yet because the blinds will get to you first, you will go broke before he does if neither of you play a hand. In that case you should consider yourself as having the smaller stack.)

How far you take this depends on the exact chip situation. For instance, if there is $100,000 in total buy-ins, eight players left, the shortest stack has $1,000, you have $1,500, and the next player has $7,000, that would be different than if the three stacks were $4,000, $5,000, and $6,000, and you had the $5,000. In the first case, you have very little chance of moving into sixth place no matter what you do. So if there is a significant difference between seventh and eighth, you should try as best you can to ensure seventh. That means throwing away all but the very best hands.

The second situation is different. If you see that the shortest stack of $4,000 is playing incredibly tight, you could match that tightness and again have a very good chance to come in seventh. But the cost is too high. With sixth place only $1,000 ahead of you, and with you possessing 5 percent of the total chips, anteing your money off to preserve seventh would be a shameful way to play. You could still easily come in sixth or higher by playing normally. Let that $4,000 stack succeed in outlasting you once in awhile. Who cares about him? There is too much money to be won for you to give it all up, just to try to outlast him.

When you have the smallest stack, the situation is the opposite. You should usually gamble, or at least not play any tighter than normal. This is especially true if you have enough chips to give you an outside chance to get lucky and win a high prize. But even if you don't have that many chips, it is more likely than not that the player who has the second smallest stack is waiting for you to go broke. So there is no point in waiting yourself. You can't outlast him.

For example, in limit hold 'em if you're the second shortest, stack don't even consider playing

if three to the right of the button. But if the smallest stack doubles up to pass you, this becomes a raising hand if first in, especially if your recent play was very tight.

Sometimes, of course, you will find yourself against a player with a slightly larger stack, who, for whatever reason, is disregarding you and still taking chances. Against him, you should often revert to the strategy of the second largest stack, play extra tightly, and hope to sneak ahead of him. This is even more true in no-limit or pot-limit tournaments, where you might get lucky enough to witness a confrontation between two of the bigger stacks, which will move you up the prize ladder.

Disregarding the above exception, the complete turnaround in strategy from the next to smallest stack to the smallest stack, can reap some unexpected benefits. I have sometimes found myself at the last table in a tournament, possessing the next to smallest stack, playing quite tightly, and making an impression on all of my opponents. But most of them simply assume that I am trying to last. Then, the lowest stack doubles up. At that point I have the shortest stack, and I immediately start raising with far more hands. And those opponents who are not aware of what we have just been discussing have no idea that I have just significantly loosened up my playing requirements, and thereby quickly throw away all but their best hands. This often allows me to steal my way back into next to last position, whence I go back into my cocoon until the shorter stack goes broke or doubles up yet again.

Down to Two Players

If you are lucky enough to be one of the last two players, it is important that you don't relax, savor your score, and play less than your best. However, the truth is that your best will usually only give you a slight advantage. That is because the stakes are so high compared to the number of chips in play.

In most tournaments the stakes move up faster than the number of players move down, so by the time it is heads-up, losing two or three pots in a row that go all the way to the river will certainly eliminate the shorter stack. Because of that, you may want to make a deal using the simple formula I outlined in the chapter on that subject.

If you don't make a deal, should you change your strategy from typical heads-up games because this is a tournament? It depends on your skill level compared to your opponent's. If you know he is better than you, you must be aggressive. Do not try to "box" with him. Instead, go for a knock-out punch. If you're the better player, you should play your normal game, except you should try to avoid playing big pots with close decisions. Again though, these recommendations will have only a minor impact on your chances. The only major mistake you could make, if you are not used to playing heads-up, is to play so tightly that you are destined to be ground down from ante steals.

When I won the "World Championship" of Draw Poker, I found myself playing heads-up against a man who would not call my opening pot-size bet unless he had a pair of sevens or better. That meant he was throwing away his hand two out of three times before the draw. I was getting even money on my opening bet. That meant it was correct for me to open with any five cards. The fact that he would call only a third of the time made my eventual victory such a certainty that I would have avoided playing a giant pot, even with four of a kind.

Actually, I did not open with every single hand because I was petrified that he would start to realize how wrong he was to fold small pairs. So, I gave him the ante once in awhile.

I tell you this story to illustrate the one catastrophic strategy that you might use if you are not accustomed to heads-up poker, and get down to the last two players. Any other reasonable strategy will find you winning this tournament with a probability close to your percentage of the total chips.

Three Illustrative Plays

Here are three examples of good tournament plays that would be debatable in a side game.

Example No. 1: Limit hold 'em. You are in the big blind with

Three people limp in, the small blind folds, and you check. The flop is

Everyone checks. The next card is the 8♦. Everyone checks. The last card is the 4♥.

This is a very good bluffing opportunity. You are risking one big bet to win four and a half small ones. You are getting a little bit better than 2-to-1. In a situation like this your chances of succeeding ought to be at least 40 percent.

The other players know that you might well have an eight and cautiously checked it on fourth street, or even have sandbagged with a jack. There does not seem to be enough money in the pot to try to keep you honest, especially in a tournament. Normally suspicious players who might call you in a side game, will throw away a hand like ace high or even two fives without a second thought. In general, stealing small pots on the last or next to last round when it seems like your opponents are weak, is much more likely to be worth the risk in a tournament than in a side game.

Example No. 2: Razz (seven-card lowball). With four low cards behind you, you raise with a

A four calls you. All others fold. You catch a jack and he catches a queen. In a tournament you should usually check (while you should probably bet in a side game).

There is no chance that he will fold, and your edge is small enough that it is probably not worth pushing. A bet on your part hurts him, but probably hurts you as well. The gainers are the other players (especially late in the tournament). When you check, it makes it easy to fold on fifth street if he catches a small one and you catch a big one. It also may allow you to win without a fight if you catch something like a seven and he catches an eight. Remember that in tournaments, winning pots immediately, rather than having merely a good chance to win a bigger pot, is usually preferred when you are one of the best players. Finally, your check may make him suspicious that your original raise might have been with a somewhat weak hand. A fact you may be able to take advantage of later.

I would caution, however, that you do not take this principle to too great an extreme. In the example given, had you caught a ten instead of a jack, you would be wrong to check.

Example No. 3: No-limit hold 'em — third level. Five people limp in before the flop. You are the big blind holding

As long as nobody is near all-in, you should seriously consider a large raise. If, for instance, the blinds are $50 and $100, a $700 to $1,000 raise would be about right. Obviously if you are reraised you don't even think of calling (although you might pretend to think). This play is okay in a side game as well, as long as you don't do it too often, but is better yet in a tournament.

It is true that some players' starting hands will tend to be a bit better in tournaments than in side games, but it doesn't matter because they are still less likely to call a big raise if their hands are merely good. This is especially true if that big raise is a reasonable percentage of their stack.

In the example given I'm assuming that your raise is at least ten percent of your opponents' stacks. (Otherwise their high implied odds might temp them.) On the other hand, it should be less than 50 percent, otherwise someone may decide to go all-in with a mediocre hand, like

or

which would be a disaster for you.

This example brings up an important concept about no-limit hold 'em, both tournaments and side games. That concept is that if you raise in no-limit, especially before the flop, you should do it only when you don't mind a reraise.

But when I say "mind" I mean that in two possible different ways. You might not mind it because your hand is so good that you will welcome it, but you also might not mind it because you would have no misgivings about folding if you get reraised. That is obviously the situation with J♠5♣. Yet almost all players, except no-limit hold 'em experts, don't understand this. They are much more apt to make the play that I suggested with a hand like

or

That is very wrong. These are two hands that would very much mind being reraised. The reason of course, is that calling that reraise is very costly and probably incorrect, while folding means you missed out on decent chances to make a hand that might very well have won a big chunk from that reraiser or others.

So again, do not raise in no-limit hold 'em, especially tournaments, if there is a reasonable chance that a reraise will make you throw up. For those of you interested in learning more about no-limit hold 'em theory, I recommend my book (co-written with Ed Miller) *No-Limit Hold 'em: Theory and Practice.* (And keep in mind there will be a lot of no-limit hold 'em stuff in "Part Five: Additional No-Limit Hold 'em Concepts" starting on page 213.)

Rebuy Tournaments

This book was written mainly to show you how to adjust from your normal winning strategies when you are playing in a poker tournament. But these new strategies assume that a player is eliminated when he goes broke. Some tournaments allow you to buy in again, after you go broke, at least during the first few hours. These are called "rebuy tournaments," and are quite common in the small buy-in, weekly tournaments. Even some events in the big tournaments, like the World Series of Poker, allow rebuys.

Besides letting you buy in two or more times when you go broke, many of these tournaments also allow you to "add-on" even if you are not broke. This option also expires after a few hours.

Because so many of your strategy changes in a tournament relate to the avoidance of being eliminated, (either yours or their's) much of what is in this book does not apply to rebuy tournaments *during the rebuy period*. Once that expires, however, the situation reverts back to normal, and the things we are learning here again apply. But now let us talk briefly about how you should play before the rebuy period expires, and whether you should rebuy.

In tournaments, where most people tend to rebuy if they go broke, your strategy during the rebuy period should somewhat revert back to that which you use in normal games. You would still, of course, adjust to any player who you notice is playing differently than usual ring game strategy. He may not be planning to rebuy, or is at least trying to avoid it. But it has been my experience that most players in a rebuy tournament play significantly looser before their rebuy option expires. This has obvious implications for your strategy. Most notably, it shrinks the "Gap" in your opening versus calling requirements.

By my saying that your initial strategy should be similar to normal side game strategy, you should deduce that I am assuming that you also will rebuy if *you* go broke. And, in fact, that is what I am assuming. If you are one of the better players in the tournament, how could that not be the right thing to do? Not only does your superior play make that second rebuy something with a positive EV, you also are taking advantage of the mathematical fact that smaller stacks are worth more per chip than the larger stacks, due to the prize structure.[19] (If you did not bring enough money to rebuy, you should tighten up even during the rebuy period. But not as much as you would tighten up if you were playing in a non-rebuy tournament since your opponents are apt to be opening looser.)

What about adding on? Is this the right play even if you are not broke? The answer usually depends on how well you are doing. Basically, the more chips you have, the more you would be inclined not to add-on. The exact point at which adding on would be a bad play depends on many factors, such as prize structure, your skill level, how many players are left, and the size of your stack. I think a conservative rule of thumb would be to add-on if you have less than the average number of chips at that point (after you include others' add-ons), and not otherwise. This rule is however conservative. If you play great, you can add on more liberally.

There is an obvious time you must add on. There are some tournaments (not the major ones) that charge less per chip for your add-on than they do for your original buy-in. You would have to almost always opt to purchase these cheaper chips.

Again, big money tournaments rarely offer rebuys. And even when they do, they turn into regular tournaments after two or three hours. That is why only this short section appears on the subject.

---

[19] See the chapters entitled "Chips Change Value" in "Part Two: Tournament Theory" and "Chips Changing Value in Tournaments Revisited" in "Part Three: Other Topics" on pages 43 and 113 respectively.

Satellites

A satellite is a tournament to get into a tournament. For the high buy-in tournaments, satellites are big business. Most consist of one table. Occasionally, for very high buy-in tournaments, like the $10,000 No-Limit Hold 'em World Championship at the World Series of Poker, the satellites are often multi-table events called a Super Satellite.

There is no question that you can have an edge playing a satellite. I rarely play them because I can make more money hourly rate wise by playing in the side games. However, it is a close decision, even for me, especially if I can pick and choose which satellite to play. Often participants in satellites are much weaker than opponents in a normal game.

The proper strategy for a one table satellite is somewhere between the proper strategy for a regular tournament and a side game. Because there are not large prizes for second, third, and fourth, the idea of sneaking into those places does not arise.[20] (Some one table satellites do have a small prize for second place, so on close decisions you might want to take that into account. But it is not a major aspect of your strategy.)

In theory, when there is only one winner, you should play exactly as if you were playing in a normal game. In practice, however, there are some adjustments even in a one table satellite compared to a side game. You still have to worry about the fact that you cannot buy more chips, and again we are presuming that you are just about the best player at the table. That means you should avoid gambling in close situations.[21] But they have to be

---

[20] See "Sit 'n Go Tournaments" starting on page 265 in "Part Five: Additional No-Limit Hold 'em Concepts."

[21] Again we are talking more about calling, not betting.

very close because the short time duration of a satellite does not allow for your greater skill to make as much of a difference, and therefore, you can't be throwing away most of your mildly profitable hands.

As far as taking advantage of the fact that your opponents don't want to go broke, I have found that many players in satellites really don't worry too much about it. It is important that you identify these players and contrast them with those who do worry. The idea, of course, is to determine which players to adjust the Gap Concept against, and which ones not to.

The other aspect of a satellite that differs from a side game is again, the number of hands that will be played without enough chips to bet all the way to the river. Just as in normal tournaments, good satellite players must do some research to see how hands behave in a "hot and cold" manner in order to give them their best chance.

Super satellites are almost exactly the same as normal tournaments. In fact there is one type of super satellite that forces you to sometimes play even tighter than you would in a normal tournament. I am speaking of super satellites where there are several winners, all of whom get the same prize, namely a buy-in for the big tournament. In that case, you could find yourself in a situation where it would be correct to throw every hand away, no matter what it was.

Suppose, for instance, the Super Satellite ended when there were five players left, each of whom would win a $10,000 buy-in. There are now seven players left and you are the chip leader. Three of the players are in imminent danger of going broke. What would you have to gain by playing even two aces? You are almost 100 percent guaranteed of winning your buy-in by doing nothing. Playing any hand gives you everything to lose with nothing to gain.

Super satellites often allow rebuys and add-ons. The principles involving the decision as to whether to rebuy or add-on are covered in the chapter on rebuy tournaments.

When All That Matters is Winning

This book usually assumes that you are anxious to have as great an expected value in the tournament as possible. Because of the nature of the prize structure, the best way to accomplish this dictates a strategy that does not quite give you the best chance of winning the tournament.

This sacrifice is worth it though, because of the increased chances of getting into the money. But what if you don't care about the money? Suppose your goal is merely to have the greatest possible chance of winning it all. (There are a lot of good reasons why you might feel this way.) How many of the concepts in this book would still apply?

Actually, most still would. The Gap Concept, for instance, still applies, only slightly less strongly, because it mainly relates to the other players' goals, not yours. You still will be raising with opening hands that are weaker than normal to take advantage of their propensity to fold. You will still be calling or reraising with hands that are stronger than normal because of their propensity to play tighter than normal (unless they themselves know the Gap Concept).

What about avoiding close gambles? This is not quite as true for you when winning is your only goal. For instance, you would not throw away the 54 percent shot in my mathematical example on pages 40 and 41 in hopes of sneaking into a higher place. But earlier in the tournament you might very well still fold on a close decision, even if winning was your only goal.

The reason again is we are assuming you are one of the best players. So if a close decision involves a significant portion of your chips, you should avoid it, even if you don't care about the

104

lesser prizes. You would prefer to preserve chips to let your skill have time to do its work.

One thing you might do differently is gamble in spots where only a small amount of chips are involved. For instance, you should find any excuse you can to play multiway pots, which if won, will allow you to amass many chips. You should gamble even more if you don't feel that you are one of the better players in the tournament, or if time means something to you.

To take an extreme example, suppose your heart is set on winning a World Series Bracelet. You are short stacked with 12 players left. Sneaking into the money will mean coming back to play the last table the next day. That means you can't enter the next day's tournament. In such a case you might want to take major chances with 12 players so that you either move way up in chips or go broke, allowing you to play tomorrow.

Again, I have no problem with those of you who, for whatever reason, play this way to maximize your chances of winning the tournament. The EV you cost yourself is not that much. But it isn't insignificant either. As long as you realize that, fine.

Tournament Theory

Afterthought

This section of the book showed how different tournaments can be from normal poker games. You are concerned with prize structure, chips changing value, and when your table will break up, among other things. These aren't even considerations in normal poker games.

Tournament differences impact how you should play your hands, they increase the "Gap," they force you to give up on many small edges, and frequently make overall play tighter.

However, keep in mind that there are a few spots where play may dramatically loosen. These usually occur right after an inflection point. So now the "gap" will narrow and you adjust accordingly, but now the other way.

All of this was illustrated in this section (and the preceding one), so it should now be obvious that even if you have a good understanding of poker strategy in general, but don't understand the appropriate tournament adjustments, your overall results will be marginal at best. Thus I suggest that if you are really serious about playing tournament poker, that you reread this and the previous section as many times as is necessary, until you get it.

Part Three
Other Topics

Other Topics

Introduction

The following section deals with some disparate miscellaneous topics that relate to poker tournaments. Some involve playing strategy, some don't. But they are all important.

Several times I have mentioned that *Tournament Poker for Advanced Players: Expanded Edition* has a whole new section concerning no-limit hold 'em tournaments. That's coming up and it's very important, so make sure you read it thoroughly. But this section also contains some material on no-limit hold 'em that was in the original edition. Don't skip this thinking that all of this material is also covered later on. That's not the case.

In addition, there are two chapters on what I call "The System." The first chapter was originally included just for fun. And the second System chapter was included simply because I thought of some refinements that improve on it a little bit. However, if you're studying this book and some of the other appropriate books from Two Plus Two Publishing LLC, you should be able to improve The System even further.

Nevertheless, The System does illustrate a very important aspect of no-limit hold 'em tournaments — the power of moving all-in. It can be a great equalizer, and at times can close the skill gap between the weak players and the no-limit hold 'em tournament stars.

Tournament Experts Versus Live Game Experts

It's well known that many tournament stars do poorly in side games and that some of the side game players struggle in tournaments. This book, so far, has been a discussion of the adjustments you'll need to make for tournament play. So there will be nothing new in this chapter. But I thought it would be worthwhile to give a quick summary of the required skill sets needed for the two types of competition. The more you understand these differences, the more you'll see why only a few players are truly great at both high stakes live games and high buy-in poker tournaments. In addition, this should help improve your results in both.

Let us now take a look at some of those required skills.

Live Game Skills

Live Game Skill No. 1: Beating top players playing their best. There are at least two reasons most people think that the high stakes side game pros are better than tournament pros and this is one of them. (The other is that side game pros make more money.) Tournament pros do not face a high proportion of excellent players. And those they do face are somewhat handcuffed by survival considerations as well as the fact that there are usually some bad players at the table. So a tournament pro doesn't have to adjust much if there happens to be a $1,000-$2,000 player in his game.

A big side game player on the other hand is almost always facing all good players with no constraints on them. Few can do this profitably.

Live Game Skill No. 2: Avoiding and taking advantage of tilt. Players are much less apt to go on tilt in tournaments than in side games. There are a few reasons for this. The most obvious being that the bad beats that might normally put someone on tilt have probably eliminated him from the tournament. Thus the skill of keeping yourself from going on tilt and honing in on those who have are not developed by strictly tournament pros. (In fact, some of them are legendary "tilters" in side games.) But these skills are critical in regular games, especially the big ones where much of the profit comes from catching an opponent playing worse than usual.

Live Game Skill No. 3: Reading hands when there are many possibilities. It is a lot tougher to read hands in a high stakes side game. Players are not nearly as reluctant to push the envelope with marginal hands. Obviously the more hands your opponent *might* have the harder it is to figure out which hand he really *does* have. Only the best higher stakes side games players can do this well.

Live Game Skill No. 4: Pushing small edges. There are many hands that are on the borderline between positive and negative EV. And it is not easy to recognize which of these will in fact make money. Furthermore, those that do will only make money if played skillfully. But tournament pros do not need to fully understand how to play those marginal hands and which ones they are because they usually fold them anyway since it is wrong to push small edges in tournaments. Not so in side games, especially big ones, where large edges are hard to come by. A $400-$800 player who doesn't seize a small edge when he has it will not win.

Live Game Skill No. 5: Understanding multi-way pots. There are a lot fewer multi-way pots during high buy-in tournaments than in typical side games. (The exception might be very high stakes shorthanded games.) And the correct strategy for these multi-way pots is often quite different than it is for heads-up post flop pots. Tournament pros are sometimes a little weak in correctly applying the principles of multi-way play. But they can get away with it. Not so for side game players.

Tournament Skills

Tournament Skill No. 1: Preserving chips. Since you are all done when you lose your buy-in, good players are usually making a mistake if they risk all or most of their chips with a small "edge" (especially playing no-limit with a decent sized stack). There are two reasons:

1. The reward is not really worth the risk since you are risking not only chips but also the opportunity to keep playing and extracting future edges.

2. The way prizes are handed out makes it mathematically wrong to take close gambles for big money, especially near the end of the tournament. (This is true even if you didn't play better than your average opponent.)

    Though the above concepts are very important for tournaments, I do not consider knowledge of them one of the key things that separates tournament champs from live game champs. The reason is that almost all live game experts are also quite cognizant of them when they are in a tournament.

Tournament Skill No. 2: When *not* to preserve chips. One thing the best tournament players understand better than most other pros is that things reverse regarding chip preservation when their stacks have shrunk and there is still more players to be knocked out before getting "into the money." Now you have to gamble, especially if the blinds are coming up. The point at which things change is what Dan Harrington calls the "inflection point." Be sure to read his thoughts on the subject.[22]

Tournament Skill No. 3: Expertise against moderate or poor opponents. I believe this may be the biggest single reason that some high stakes live game players do not do as well as one might expect when they play tournaments. They are not adept at extracting the maximum (or losing the minimum) when up against weak opponents. And even the highest buy-in tournaments have a good percentage of players with quite a bit less skill than the opponents that top ring players are used to playing. I'm not saying that the live game players will actually *lose* to these mediocre players. But many of them don't beat these "weakies" out of nearly as much as tournament pros do.

Tournament Skill No. 4: Taking advantage of other's "Fear of Busting Out." For the details of how to do this you'll have to read on. For now, be aware that typical players play differently in a tournament than they do in side games and the correct counter strategy is also different. Tournament pros tend to be more aware of what that strategy is. (In a nutshell it means more betting and folding, and less calling and raising [except on the first level].)

Tournament Skill No. 5: Playing with or against short stacks. This is another skill that many live game pros lack. That's not surprising of course since big games rarely contain players who allow themselves to become short. But the fact is that knowing when to go all-in on an early round, either as a bettor or a caller, is an actual skill (and a difficult one to learn) if the situation comes up frequently. So is fully understanding the ramifications of playing when there is a side pot. Live game players who don't learn this stuff are at a big disadvantage in a tournament.

---

[22] See *Harrington on Hold 'em; Expert Strategy for No-Limit Tournaments: Volume II: End Play.*

Chips Changing Value
in Tournaments Revisited

Let's revisit the idea that chips change value in tournaments. Suppose you are playing in a $100 buy-in no-limit hold 'em tournament where they give you face value, i.e one hundred dollars worth of chips to start. You double up. What has that done to your EV? Has it doubled? Or has it increased by some other amount? The answer depends on four factors:

1. How well you play in comparison to the other entrants?

2. How are the prizes distributed?

3. How close are you to the money?

4. Is $100 in tournament chips an adequate stack to allow you to wait for a truly playable hand?

Everybody knows that a large increase in stack size does not mean your EV has increased proportionally in tournaments where first place has to "give back" a lot of the money, *especially near the end*. I won't insult your intelligence with another explanation. (The one exception occurs if you are a terrible player. Which is why those players should gamble crazily, especially pre-flop in hold 'em.)

But what about when you are at the beginning or middle of a tournament? Could you be a good player, yet still be in a position where doubling up *more* than doubles your expectation? The answer is "not likely." That's true not only if there are lots of prizes, but still probably true even if the tournament is "winner take all." I'll prove that shortly.

But first I want to make something clear. Even though extra chips are almost never worth as much as already owned chips (meaning significant numbers of owned chips should not be risked on very close propositions), these extra chips can easily be worth more than their face value as long as you play well. Thus an "add-on" can be right even if it would be wrong to play a coin flip for these chips getting 11-to-10. And it is even more right if most of the other players are adding on as well.

Right that is from a purely EV standpoint. The problem is that your stack might have increased to the point where the extra chips are positively valued to a much smaller extent than your original buy-in. If so, the add on might be contraindicated due to gambler's ruin considerations.

That is one of the reasons, as we have already seen, that this text offers the conservative advice that you should add-on as long as your chips are below average.[23] For very good players who don't have bankroll considerations the threshold is higher. And of course when I speak of having average chips, I mean *after* everyone has purchased the add-on.

Now let's get back to the question of whether extra chips are worth less and how the answer should affect your tournament strategy. Earlier, I said that even in one winner tournaments the best players are usually in a situation where extra chips are worth less than owned chips (again though, still often worth more than face value). To show this, one need merely ask the question, "Is such a player favored to double up before he goes broke?" If the answer is yes, as you would expect it to be for great players, chips must lose value.

Suppose for instance that in a 32 player tournament with a total of $3,200 in tournament chips, a good player's $100 buy-in corresponding to $100 in tournament chips was worth $150. Could his doubling to $200 in tournament chips be worth $301?

---

[23] See "Rebuy Tournaments" starting on page 100 in "Part Two: Tournament Theory."

And to $400 in tournament chips, $603, and to $800 in tournament chips, $1,207? And to $1,600 in tournament chips, $2,415? And to $3,200 in tournament chips, $4,831? Obviously not.

Notice however that this proof assumes that the great player figures to double up before going broke. That is usually true. But there are exceptions. One rare one is the player who plays a lot better with a big stack. In other words he is *not* a favorite to double up *until* he has gotten a lot of chips (almost inconceivable for limit tournaments). This is sometimes the case for psychological reasons, either in his mind or his opponents. Or it might simply be that he is weak playing shorter stacks. Such a player would be well advised to gamble early in a tournament including even calling close all-in bets. Meanwhile, there is a more common situation where a good player is not favored to double up before going broke. I speak of those times where his stack is very short.

(When this occurs he may well have an EV greater than the amount of his chips. But that is only because if he does double up he is in a lot better shape.)

The reason a very short stack turns a good player into one who is no longer favored to double up before going broke is that he doesn't have enough chips to profitably wait for hands to play against the above average hands he is likely to face. On our forums at www.twoplustwo.com, Aaron Brown did a simulation on the Poker Theory Forum that makes this point clear. (He also did a simulation that convincingly demonstrates that very big stacks should not purchase add-ons.)

Now the ramifications of this fact are a bit complicated. But the bottom line is to be aware when you are in, or approaching these situations. Obviously, if your stack has gotten so low that you are more likely to go broke than double up, you should not pass up any coin flip. Furthermore, if you are just above that threshold (which seems to be about the points where it would take 30 to 40 hands to blind, or ante, you off) you must be cognizant of how soon the stakes are going up to where that same bankroll falls under the threshold.

Finally, always remember the giant differences between calling and raising, in other words, the Gap Concept, especially if your opponents are not maniacs. Even if your won chips are worth less than your owned chips, a big bet that might win immediately can be well worth it with hands that are underdogs if called. Since this is even more true in those situations where your short stack temporarily makes the second derivative of the value of your chips positive, you better be doing a lot of first to act, all-in moves, in this situation. Just like Dan Harrington and Bill Robertie in *Harrington on Hold 'em; Expert Strategy for No-Limit Tournaments; Volume II: Strategic Play* and I have already told you.

Last Longer Bets

It is a common practice among tournament players to make side bets with each other as to who will last longer in the tournament. As a general principle, these bets should not be made unless they are very small or very large.

The reason being is that you don't really want to have a moderate bet affect your tournament strategy. A hand can come up where the right play for the tournament is the wrong play for your side bet. The examples are so obvious I won't bother going into them.

Of course, if the guy who wants to make the last longer bet with you is a complete idiot, go ahead and make it, and play your normal tournament strategy. After all, that strategy, if you follow the precepts in this book, will tend to make you last longer than most.

However, it has been my experience that the only people who make these bets are those who play a conservative tournament strategy themselves. The only time you might want to bet against them is if they are willing to make a very large bet. In that case, it is worth giving up some tournament equity in order to increase the chances of winning the side bet. If you think they will not be changing their own strategy, you may have a pretty big edge on your side bet if you play super tight.

That of course will hurt your tournament chances. But if you are strictly in it for the money, the bet may be worth making. I never make such bets, and I love it when others at my table do, since it is pretty easy to take advantage of someone who you know is worried about a big last longer bet.

Of course, some people like to make small last longer bets just to keep things interesting. They have no intention of changing their strategy, but just want a little extra action. If you find such things fun, go right ahead.

Freezeout Calculations

It is a common assumption that your chances of winning a tournament against equally skilled players are equivalent to the fraction of the total tournament chips that you hold (in your stack). Thus, if you own 15 percent of the chips, your chances of winning are 15 percent. This happens to be right, even though most people don't know why. Assuming everybody is equally skilled and is playing similar strategies, the chance of each player coming in first is precisely in proportion to the size of their stacks.

For the sake of completeness, I would like to demonstrate this fact in the case of two hypothetical players. There is both a mathematical and a logical argument. Let's first do a couple of situations mathematically. (Those who hate this stuff can skip it.)

Suppose Player A has exactly three times as much as Player B. Here is a non-rigorous, but compelling, demonstration that Player A will win this freezeout three quarters of the time. First, what are the chances that Player B will double up? This is basically the same as asking for the chances that Player B will win a freezeout against someone who has the same number of chips as him. Well clearly a freezeout between two equal stacks and two equal players is a fifty-fifty proposition. But in order for Player B to win the freezeout against Player A he must double up (one-half probability) and then double up again (one-half probability). So his chances are one-half times one-half or one quarter.

$$\frac{1}{4} = \left(\frac{1}{2}\right)\left(\frac{1}{2}\right)$$

It is 3-to-1 against him or exactly the ratio of the chips.

Here's a slightly more complicated example. Suppose Player A has twice as many chips as Player B. Let us call Player A's chances of winning the freezeout X. Player B's chances are therefore (1-X). For Player B to win he must first double up, which will give him twice as many chips as Player A, after which he must win a second freezeout where it is he who has twice the chips. So his chances (1-X) require a parlay, the first part of which has a probability of one-half and the second part which has a probability of X (because he is now in exactly the same situation as A originally was). Thus 1-X equals one-half times X.

$$1 - X = \left(\frac{1}{2}\right)X$$

Therefore X equals two-thirds.

$$1 - X = \left(\frac{1}{2}\right)X \Rightarrow$$
$$2 - 2X = X \Rightarrow$$
$$2 = 3X \Rightarrow$$
$$X = \frac{2}{3}$$

Again notice that this corresponds to the ratio of the chips.

There is, however, a more elegant, purely logical proof that equal players in a symmetrical situation must win exactly in proportion to the size of their stacks. Suppose these two players agreed to play the same freezeout everyday for ten years. Given they are equal players, their long run results would necessarily be to break even. Well in order for them to break even, the smaller stack must win exactly the same fraction of times as the fraction of the total chips he possesses. This reasoning extends to any number of players as long as they play equally well, and there is no positional advantage for one compared to the other.

Unfortunately, there is no equally simple technique to calculate the chances of coming in second, third, etc. based solely on the chip count. There are, however, some good ways of estimating these probabilities. (See *Gambling Theory and Other Topics* by Mason Malmuth for further discussion.)

Making Deals

If you are lucky enough to get down to the last two players, you may want to make a deal with your opponent. At this point you are probably playing such high stakes that two or three pots will decide the winner. Meanwhile, the money involved is going to be much more than you are used to playing for. As long as your opponent is also inclined to make a deal, you can probably agree without giving up anything. In other words, he will probably be willing to give you a fair deal, or maybe even one that is mathematically advantageous to you.

With only two players left, calculating what you have coming if you ended the tournament immediately is pretty simple. However, the calculation does assume that both players are equal. If you feel like you are clearly the superior player, you might want to get more than the value that these calculations would show.

Keep in mind, however, that your playing superiority probably counts for very little, due to the size of the stakes compared to the stacks, unless your edge comes from the fact that he folds too much. (If that is the case, you can rob him a little at a time, even at these high stakes, and may in fact have a much greater chance than the chip ratios would indicate, especially if you have enough chips to withstand losing a pot.)

You also might shoot for more if you know your opponent is hard up for money, or if you know that he does not know how to calculate the fair price himself. That is up to you.

In the preceeding chapter we showed that with equal players the probability that one player wins is exactly in proportion to his chips. Thus, in a heads-up contest, the player with 60 percent of the chips has a 60 percent chance of winning. With this in mind, it is easy to figure out how much two players should settle for if they want to make a deal and stop the tournament (or perhaps continue playing, but only for the "title").

There are two ways to do this. Suppose first prize is $20,000 and second prize is $12,000. Again we will say that one player has 60 percent of the chips, while the other has 40 percent. The straightforward way to calculate what each player is entitled to is to compute their expected value. The way you do that is you multiply each of the prizes times the chances of winning it. And then you add up those numbers. In this case the leader has a 60 percent chance of winning $20,000, which multiplies to $12,000

$$\$12,000 = (.60)(\$20,000)$$

and a 40 percent chance of winning $12,000, which multiplies to $4,800

$$\$4,800 = (.40)(\$12,000)$$

Add them up. That's $16,800.

$$\$16,800 = \$12,000 + \$4,800$$

The other player has a 40 percent chance for $20,000, which is $8,000, and a 60 percent chance of $12,000, which is $7,200. That adds up to $15,200. Notice that the two figures add up to the proper amount, namely $32,000.

$$\$32,000 = \$16,800 + \$15,200$$

The above method is perfectly fine, and when there are more than two players involved, it is the one you should use. But with only two players, there is an even simpler one.

Notice that at this point the two players are fighting for $8,000, since second place prize money is guaranteed to both of them. The chip leader should win that $8,000 60 percent of the time. He is therefore entitled to $4,800 of that $8,000.

$$\$4,800 = (.60)(\$8,000)$$

The other player is entitled to 40 percent of the $8,000, which is $3,200.

$$\$3,200 = (.40)(\$8,000)$$

The leader should therefore get the $12,000 second prize, plus another $4,800, which is $16,800. The other guy should get 40 percent of that $8,000, or $3,200, plus the second prize of $12,000, which is $15,200. This, of course, is the same answer we got before.

In the case of three players, we cannot be so precise. The reason is that there is no ironclad way to calculate the chances of coming in second and third based on your chip position. Your chances of winning are still the same as the ratio of your chips (with equal players). It is also obvious that the player who has the least chips has the greatest chance of coming in third. But the exact probabilities depend on how the hands are being played, and specifically, how often multiway pots are being played.

In spite of this lack of precision, you should have a pretty good idea of what you should settle for simply using some common sense. Suppose Player A has $12,000 in chips, Player B has $6,000 in chips, and Player C has $2,000 in chips. Now if this was a one winner tournament, where the winner simply got $20,000, the proper settlement would be just exactly how much they had in front of them, namely, $12,000, $6,000, and $2,000. But the prize structure changes that significantly.

Suppose first prize is $8,000, second prize is $5,000, and third prize is $3,000. Let's look at Player C, the guy with the short stack. His chances of winning are simply his proportion of the chips, namely one-tenth or 10.0 percent.

$$10.0 = \left(\frac{1}{10}\right)(100)$$

But what about his chances of coming in second? Although not perfectly accurate, we can estimate how likely it is that he beats out Player B, the second place man. Since Player B has three times as many chips, Player C has about a 1-in-4 chance of doing that. Since we already gave Player C a 10.0 percent chance of winning, this gives him about a 22.5 percent chance of coming in second

$$22.5 = \left(\frac{1}{4}\right)(100 - 10.0)$$

and thus he comes in 3rd the remaining 67.5 percent of the time or so.

$$67.5 = 100 - 10.0 - 22.5$$

It is now simply a matter of multiplying expectations.

$$\$800 = (.100)(\$8,000)$$

$$\$1,125 = (.225)(\$5,000))$$

$$\$2,025 = (.675)(\$3,000)$$

When you add those numbers up you get $3,950.

$$\$3,950 = \$800 + \$1,125 + \$2,025$$

Does this surprise you? This seems like quite a bit for a guy with only $2,000 in (tournament) chips. Then again, realize that he had $3,000 guaranteed to him.

The truth is, that in most three-way settlements, the third guy tends to shortchange himself. On the other hand, he might have difficulty getting what he deserves because the other two guys are miscalculating also. The best way to take advantage of this misunderstanding is to wait until you are the chip leader, or close to it in a three- or four-way finish, especially if the shorter stacks are small, but not tiny.[24] They present more of a danger than most people realize. And you are likely to be able to get a settlement that is better for you than it appears.

One final note. There are a few people out there who would much rather win the tournament than win the money. In these cases deals have been made where the "second place finisher" got much the best of it in terms of money.

In the past, there has been some questioning on the ethics of this type of deal and I'm not going to comment one way or the other about it.[25] However, if you manage to get heads-up at the final table, and one of you is only interested in the money, and the other is anxious for the title, a very favorable deal for both parties can sometimes be made.

---

[24] This is exactly the opposite of other authors' advice which recommend striving for a deal when you are short stacked but not otherwise. They are wrong.

[25] I wrote this in the first edition. Now I must add that any deals like this are completely unethical if any "all around" prizes could be affected.

Some No-Limit Observations

Note: The next few chapters, mainly about no-limit hold 'em tournaments, were part of the first edition. Later on there will be a larger section on these tournaments that were written only for the expanded edition.

The only tournaments that are offered no-limit style are hold 'em, and sometimes lowball. No-limit lowball will not be discussed here since it is offered so infrequently. But no-limit hold 'em is a common tournament event. In fact, it can be found more often in tournaments than as a side game.[26] The final event of most major tournament gatherings is usually a high buy-in no-limit hold 'em event. The "World Poker Champion" is the winner of the final event at the World Series of Poker, the $10,000 No-Limit Hold 'em World Championship.

As a general rule, no-limit hold 'em tournaments are the most profitable for the best players. In a 200 player event, excellent players may have as great as a 1-in-50 chance of winning, and an expected profit as high as four times their buy-in. Such a situation cannot occur in any limit tournament. One reason for the no-limit expert's tournament edge is simply that no-limit is not played by everyone outside of tournaments, so the top players are facing many neophytes, who are just taking a shot.[27] And, as a general rule, an inexperienced no-limit player will tend to get destroyed by an experienced one.

---

[26] This statement, while still accurate, is now somewhat misleading. With the poker boom that began when the first TV shows appeared in 2003, the predominant game, in both tournaments and side games, is now no-limit hold 'em.

[27] Again, not nearly as true as it once was.

In other words, a major reason why no-limit tournaments are so profitable to the experts is that they get a chance to play against so many significantly inferior players. This does not occur in limit events where even the typical player plays pretty well.

There are other reasons besides expertise in no-limit which makes these tournaments great for the "cream of the crop." What I'm referring to is expertise in no-limit tournament strategy. And I am not only talking about the Gap Concept. It is still important, but only as it applies to larger opening bets. In that case, you again need a much bigger hand to call with than you would need to open with. However, if the opening bet is small, that might not be true. If you are one of the better players, you can play a lot of hands when its cheap to come in because of the edges you can obtain from future bets.

Another aspect of tournament strategy that applies especially to no-limit are the adjustments you make depending on the size of your own and your opponents' stack. For instance, it is much more important to avoid marginal confrontations against good players with larger stacks in no-limit than it is in limit. It is also easier to take advantage of moderately small stacks that are trying to survive since they know you can bust them in one hand.[28] Finally, your knowledge of all-in prices is rewarded more in no-limit than in a limit game since all-in situations and decisions as to whether to call all-in or raise someone else all-in come up much more often.

Don't Turn Good Hands Into Seven-Deuce

Elsewhere in this book I describe a couple of seemingly strange plays that I say are worth making. One involves a big raise

---

[28] See Question 48 of the "Hand Quizzes" on page 208 for an example.

before the flop with a lousy hand. The other involves checking top pair and the nut flush draw on fourth street in last position.[29] In both spots, I give a brief explanation of an important no-limit concept. But I want to repeat it here as well.

General poker theory teaches that someone who makes a bet or raise into us, hurts us the most when we have a close decision as far as whether or not to call. Certainly when someone bets or raises in a spot where we know that we probably have a better hand than they do, we welcome that action. Almost as obvious is the fact that when their bet or raise indicates we have no chance of having the best hand or even of drawing out, that bet or raise does not hurt since we fold. It may even help since we avoid committing further chips down the road.

What is less obvious is that, when someone forces us to call when we are probably beaten, or forces us to fold when we still had a decent chance of winning, it is quite bad. And it's especially bad in no-limit where a person can bet or raise specifically the amount that puts maximum pressure on us. The upshot of all of this is that it is often advisable to refrain from giving your opponent the opportunity to apply this pressure when we have a hand that has decent chances of winning.

What this means is that with such hands we should usually avoid raising or check raising since that will open up the possibility of getting reraised. It also means strongly considering checking in last position hands that will hate getting check raised. Again, when I say "hate," I mean being put in a position where your hand may still win, but not often enough where you will welcome that raise, yet not rarely enough where you can happily fold against it. Notice that this concept may not apply to those times you are in first position since you don't end the betting round if you check.

---

[29] See Question 27 of the "Hand Quizzes" on page 183 for an example.

The reason for this section's title is that beginning no-limit players make a common mistake, putting in fairly big bets or raises before the flop with hands that are very good, but not so good as to welcome a reraise. The problem is that these big bets will almost never be flat called.

Usually they will steal the pot. Maybe even often enough to show a profit. But when they don't, they get reraised big time. So big that you usually have to fold. But that is very sad when your hand is something like

or

with lots of chips in front of you. These are hands that might have won a big pot had you not played them that way.

Yes, it's true that a raise might win the pot instantly often enough to make it worth doing. If so, go ahead and do it with seven-deuce, not ace-queen suited. Either way you will have to fold if reraised. But if you do it with ace-queen, you have in fact, made it no better than seven-deuce. And this principle applies to later rounds as well.

Ace-King in No-Limit

The specific hand, ace-king, in the specific game, no-limit hold 'em, deserves some special attention.

In limit hold 'em, ace-king is a very good, but not great hand, especially when it is not suited. But what about no-limit hold 'em? Does its value go up or down when compared to the limit game?

The answer is actually both. When you have lots of money in front of you, ace-king can be a very tricky hand to play in no-limit, because, when you get involved, you usually have made only one pair. Of course that pair is top pair with the best kicker, which, in a limit game, is all you ever need to eventually win all the money. But in no-limit, that same hand can get you into trouble. Weaker players will tend to win a little with it frequently, but sometimes lose a lot with it. And those losses might add up to more than the wins.

But there is another aspect to ace-king in no-limit. That is, if you get all-in with it before the flop, you are almost never in bad shape. The math is simple. Against a pocket pair below kings, your chances are just a tad less than even money. Against two undercards, you are well over 60 percent. Against an ace or king and an undercard you're 75 percent. The only real disaster is if you are against two aces. Now you are less than 10 percent to win. Even against two kings you are about 30 percent.

Put another way, ace-king has at least three reasons to prefer to be all-in before the flop in a no-limit game:

1. It will sometimes be the best hand, even without improving, when all the cards are out. However, many of the times that it would wind up the best hand unpaired, it has been forced to fold by a bettor. Unless, of course, it was all-in.

2. Most of the time that ace-king wins, it is with one pair — a hand that is very tricky to play in no-limit hold 'em, especially to those who are not used to playing that game.

3. A large percentage of the time that ace-king wins a showdown will be when it catches an ace or a king on fourth or fifth street. However, if it is not all-in, it will often not be around to catch those cards since in no-limit, a bet on the flop is rarely worth calling with merely two overcards.

Thus, we see that moving in before the flop with ace-king is often the best way to play this hand. It is important to understand, however, that it is a lot better to be the bettor when you put all your money in, rather than calling someone else's all-in bet. This is especially true in a tournament where players are apt to throw away some pretty good hands in the face of your all-in bet or raise, including hands that they would have moved in with had they acted before you.

For instance, suppose a typical player might make a big bet, putting you or himself all-in, with a pair of nines or better, as well as ace-king. But if you move in, he will call with only queens or better, and maybe ace-king suited. Against a player like this, your results improve quite a bit if you are the aggressor since you win the pot immediately against three hands (nines, tens, or jacks) that are a favorite over you.

Contrast this with those times you have a pair of pocket jacks against this same opponent. With two jacks, you are better off being the caller because you don't want nines and tens to fold. In general, jacks are a better hand than ace-king offsuit. But usually not when they are used as move in hands.

Let's say once you move in you will only be called by two aces, two kings, or two queens. If you move in with two jacks, your chances are only about 17 percent (when you are called) since that is your approximate chance against each of these three overpairs.

When you have ace-king, you will be about 45 percent against queens, about 30 percent against kings, and about 9 percent against aces. However, since aces and kings are half as likely as queens, given your hole cards, (three combinations each versus six combinations for the queens) your total chances of winning are around 30 percent, which is a lot better than a pair of jacks' chances.

$$0.3 = \frac{(6)(.45) + (3)(.30) + (3)(.09)}{12}$$

The jacks catch up only if there is a possibility they are facing tens or worse. (Admittedly a definite possibility in many situations, especially late in the tournament.)

Of course, this example is postulating a situation where you have only a 30 percent chance of winning when you move in with ace-king, which might make you wonder how it could be a good play. The answer, of course, is that the play will win the pot without a fight very often, which is the largest aspect to making this a profitable play. Your 30 percent chance of winning when you are called is, however, also often needed to make the play an overall positive EV move.

Notice that ace-queen is quite a bit worse off than ace-king if one of the possible calling hands for the opponent is ace-king, as well as the three highest pairs. Not only is ace-queen a big underdog to ace-king, it is also twice as likely to run into a pair of kings. Thus, moving in with ace-queen is not nearly as advantageous as doing it with ace-king.

The best time to move in with ace-king is when moving in is betting two to fives times the size of the pot. When the bet is smaller than this, especially when someone else has already bet, you will almost always get called. That means you do not have the two ways to win that you normally would. That makes your move-in bet equivalent to merely calling. It still might be right to do, but your EV is a lot less since you could be running into small pairs that would have folded to a bigger raise.

Raising or betting more than five times the size of the pot is also a debatable play, not because it won't usually win, but because you might be risking too much to win too little. If raising three times the pot will guarantee your opponent has queens or better when he calls, then raising five times the pot does you little extra good.

Keep this in mind, however. If your stack size is such that you have, say, seven times what's in the pot, there is little point in raising only four times the pot to save money, because anyone who does play with you will almost certainly move you the rest of the way in. Thus, you may as well have moved in yourself. If you do have significantly more than five times the pot, and look down and see ace-king, you may decide that it is better to just call or perhaps raise a small enough amount that you can fold if reraised.

Many of these decisions will depend on how well you play no-limit hold 'em compared to your opponents. Unless you are easily the best player, you might decide to make ace-king an almost automatic move-in hand anytime it has a chance of winning the pot immediately, regardless of the size of the pot. One other advantage to this style is that if you show the hand, it will allow you to do the same thing with a pair of aces, which now might get a call from hands that would have otherwise folded, had they not seen your ace-king move.

Of course, if you do choose to move in with most of your ace-kings, you are choosing to play a style that can get you broke instantly. That goes against some general precepts of tournament play. So don't do it if you know you are the best player, and your chips are many times the size of the pot. And if you do decide that you like being all-in with ace-king before the flop, make sure that's more likely to occur because you are betting as opposed to calling.

When You are Not the Best Player

In general, this book has assumed that you play as well as the best players in the tournament, and better than the rest. But what if you don't? While this possibility will not be addressed in regard to other games, it could be relevant to no-limit. Suppose, for instance, it occurs that you are better than the average player, but definitely not as good as the top players in the tournament.

If this was a pot-limit, rather than a no-limit tournament, the overall situation would be unprofitable. The edge you have against the bad players would not make up for your disadvantage against the best ones. But no-limit is different. Why? Because you can easily get all-in before the flop.

It turns out that a willingness to do this can be a tremendous thorn in the side of a top player. With the exception of two aces, no starting hand can ever feel that comfortable if all the money goes in before the flop. And, if you feel like you are playing against better players, you can take advantage of this fact.

A Proposition

Suppose I walk up to a world champion hold 'em player and offer him the following proposition: A heads-up $5,000 no-limit hold 'em freezeout. We play until one of us has the whole $10,000. The blinds are $100 on the button, and $200 in front of the button. But now I add a little wrinkle. I will move in all of my chips before the flop every hand! It doesn't matter what I have. Clearly, my opponent has an edge. But how big is it?

Suppose I tell him I will play this freezeout if he doubles my win when I win. In other words, he pays me a total of $10,000 those times I win, while I lose only $5,000 when I don't. Should he accept?

Believe it or not, the answer is definitely no. Even if he plays perfectly, he will win this freezeout only about 60 percent of the time. With a little thought you should be able to see why he can't lay 2-to-1.

Let's look at this a little closer. Suppose, for instance, on the first hand he is dealt

What should he do? That hand is a favorite against my two random cards, but the problem is that it is not a 2-to-1 favorite. The actual percentage is 57 percent. Thus, if he calls my bet he is laying 2-to-1 on a 57-to-43 or 1.33-to-1 shot. So it would seem like he needs to wait until he has a hand that is much more of a favorite than this one.

The problem, of course, is that he is being ground down while he is waiting. So when he finally does get a good enough hand to play, (which by the way would be a hand that has a less than 66 percent chance once chips are not even) he not only risks going broke on that hand, he also leaves you with chips, sometimes a significant number of them, even when he wins the confrontation.

The point is that no-limit hold 'em, with all of its skill, is a game where a very aggressive pre-flop strategy can largely negate that skill. It is like a boxing match where you find yourself against a better fighter. *In* such a case, since you have little chance of winning a 10 or 12 round decision, you are better off going for a knock-out punch, even if that is not your normal style.

The "System"

To show how effective moving in before the flop against good players is, I relate the following true story. A well known casino owner wanted to give his 21 year old daughter the thrill of playing in the final world championship event at the World Series of Poker at Binion's Horseshoe in Las Vegas. He was perfectly ready to put up the $10,000 for her to play in that no-limit event. There was only one problem. She had never played poker in her life.

There was a week to go before the tournament, and he approached me to give her lessons. I appreciated his confidence, but taking someone who has never played poker before and turning them into a champion no-limit player in a week, is an impossible task. Even for me.

However, I did have an idea. I had been mulling over the concept of doing a lot of moving in before the flop. A few years earlier a very mediocre poker player had won the World Championship making great use of this play. Upon reflection I realized that he had hit upon a strategy which gave him almost as good a chance as the best players. In fact, if those players did not properly adjust to it, he might even have an edge over them. This is especially true because the best players hate to go all-in before the flop, even if they suspect they have a small edge by doing so. They would much rather spar than slug it out. That is, they want to wait for a situation they are almost sure about, rather than speculating that they have the best of it.

Getting back to the casino owner's daughter, I came up with a plan (which the casino owner dubbed "The System") that would take advantage of the above syndrome, and actually give her a chance. Amazingly, this system did not even require that she know how to play poker, or even what beat what. All it required her to do was to move in or fold. (There was a slight problem when she

136

had the big blind. I found a way to deal with that, but we will ignore it to simplify this story.)

The instructions that I gave her, to the best of my recollection, were the following:

1.   If someone else has raised in front of you, move in all of your chips with aces, kings, or ace-king suited. Otherwise fold.

2.   If no one else has raised in front of you, move in all your chips with any pair, any ace-other suited, ace-king (suited or offsuit), or two suited connected cards, except for four-trey or trey-deuce.

That was basically the whole system. The only other thing besides a separate instruction for the big blind, was that this system was not to be used the first few rounds of the tournament.

The reason The System wasn't to be used at first was that there was too little money in the pot. The $10,000 No-Limit Hold 'em World Championship at the World Series of Poker used to start off with blinds of $25 and $50. If she were to move in $10,000, she would be destined to run into a pair of aces well before she had stolen enough antes. Thus, even if all her opponents would throw anything but aces away, The System would be obviously wrong to use when the blinds were that small. So, for the first two or three levels her instructions were different. They were to throw everything away except aces, and to move in with those aces.

Obviously, The System (of selective moving in before the flop) could have been fine tuned further. For instance, I could have adjusted for her position, or whether somebody had already limped in front of her.[30] But I was dealing with someone *who had never played poker* and didn't want to make things more

---

[30] See the next chapter "Improving The "System" starting on page 142.

complicated. In spite of this, we actually felt like The System, as it stood, still gave her a chance.

Notice that the hands that she was to move in with (again, when no one raised in front of her) comprised about 13 percent of all the two card combinations. (If you don't know how I got that, stop reading this book right now. You are not ready for it. You don't know enough about poker. And, you deserve to lose.) That means that if she got away with her raises, even if she only stole the ante, her stack would gradually go up since she was raising often enough to recapture her blinds plus a little more.[31] And of course, there was no reason why she could not get called and still win. In general, if she did get called, she would probably be an underdog, but rarely a big underdog.

I was also counting on the fact that other players were worried about going broke and also about players yet to act behind them. I had little doubt that, if she raised in an early position, players on her immediate left would fold hands as good as

or maybe even

---

[31] Of course this assumes a full table. If she got lucky enough to get down to a few players she wouldn't be playing enough hands. That flaw is remedied in the improved system that follows in the next chapter.

or

and, this in fact did happen.

The big problem of course, is that she would eventually run into aces. There were only two ways to withstand that. One, was to beat those aces — most of the hands she would be raising with were about 20 percent against them. The other possibility would be that the player with aces had less money than she did, so she would still have chips to build back up. Because her ante stealing and possible pot winning would mean that her stack was increasing, it was quite reasonable that she would still be alive when she finally did lose to two aces.

Thus, The System, even though it is quite simplistic, actually seemed like it would give her a chance. The math seemed to work out, and there wasn't much that expert players could do to counter it. (As an aside, notice that if I was right, you could argue that it is a *knock* on no-limit tournaments that such a simple system could negate all the weapons of the best players.)[32]

So how did she end up? Before I tell you, I must tell you about the tournament that occurred the day before the big one. That was also a no-limit event. It had a much smaller buy-in, perhaps $2,000. Because it was a one day event, the blinds started off proportionately much higher. An ante was also added after the first couple of levels. The casino owner, skeptical of my system, decided to test it himself in this smaller tournament. To make a

---

[32] Unfortunately, I believe this is true, which is why I have been an advocate of changing the World Championship event to a multi-game format.

long story short, The System brought his chips from $2,000 to $35,000! He made the final table, and came in about fifth place. But even that does not properly describe the result, because for some reason, with $35,000 in chips, he decided, for the first time in the tournament, to deviate from The System. Specifically, what he did was call a raise in front of him with

The flop came

and the raiser had two tens. Furthermore, the raiser was the only player who had more chips than he did. Thus there is every reason to believe that had he followed The System, he would have come in at least the top three.

His daughter was not so lucky. After anteing off about $2,000 in the first few levels, The System kicked in and she began increasing her chips. Players were throwing jacks and queens away in the face of her all-in raise, just as expected. She was called one time by ace-king, and won with her pair. But alas, right near the end of the first day, she ran into a big stack with the dreaded aces. I always wonder what would have happened had she won that hand.

Except for confiding in a few friends, I have never told or written about this system before. I am extremely curious as to how

The "System" 141

strong it really might be. And if it is strong, how much stronger yet a more complex, move all-in, system would be? Most good players would feel very silly playing such a system, so anyone who tested it would more likely be a gambler who does not have his ego involved. Now that I have divulged it, I expect a few of you might give it a try.

One thing is for sure, if you do get into a big tournament and use it, it won't matter much that others know your strategy. There is no good counter strategy which avoids significant risk. In fact, if you use it at a table with some famous world champions, I guarantee you will have them tearing their hair out.

Since the first edition of this book, I have dabbled with a system that takes into account the important factors that the original system ignores: Stack size, blind size, number of limpers, number of players yet to act.

I wrote an article describing a (still far from perfect) way to incorporate this information into a bit more complicated move in system. Here is a reprint of that article.

Improving The "System"

In my book, *Tournament Poker for Advanced Players,* I recount an experience I had regarding the World Series of Poker $10,000 Championship Event. A wealthy casino owner wanted to give his daughter a thrill by staking her in the tournament. Unfortunately, she had never played a hand of poker of any type.

I was given the assignment to prepare her in only a few hours. It seemed like an impossible task. But I got a flash of inspiration. I realized that no-limit hold 'em allowed for a super simple strategy that wasn't all that bad. Namely, either folding or moving in before the flop. Considering the tremendous pressure this would put on other players, especially in a tournament, I might just be able to devise a method that would at least give her a chance.

My book describes The System in more detail, but essentially I had her moving in with any pair, any suited connector, and with ace-king. Everything else she folded. The day before the big tournament the casino owner came in fifth place in a smaller no-limit event by following the same System. Unfortunately, in his daughter's case, she ran into pocket aces late on the first day's play and was eliminated, after holding her own for six hours.

The reason why the simple System has a chance, is twofold.

1.   Most opponents will not jeopardize their whole stack in close situations (e.g. with two jacks or ace-queen), thereby allowing The System player to steal a lot of small pots.

2.   I chose hands that had a decent chance to win when they were called.

But the simple System had at least two obvious problems. They are:

1.   It did not take into account stack size versus blind size.

2.   It did not take into account how many players were yet to act.

If the rest of the table merely waited for aces, that would probably be good enough to thwart the System at the beginning of the tournament, where moving in was risking so much to win so little. Conversely, if the System player was lucky enough to reach the final five, he or she would be folding so many hands that the blinds would eat them up even if they were never called.

There was no way I had time to teach her anything other than the simplest System, drawbacks and all. However, I realized the System could easily be improved to avoid a lot of these drawbacks. I wasn't willing to do the advanced analysis to make a move or fold system anywhere near perfect (I invite others to improve The System further.) But realized that some reasonable rules of hand selection that take stack size and position into account would go a long way to making System players much harder to contend with.

Before explaining the improved System, I must point out that there is one situation it doesn't cover. I speak of the times you are in the big blind and nobody raises. You might also include the times you are in the small blind and decide to flick in a chip to call. What you do in these situations is up to you. If you think you play well, then go ahead and play it normally. (But if you lose a lot of chips on those hands you will always wonder what would have happened if you didn't.) If you choose to go to the other extreme you could move in if the flop makes you the nuts and check fold if you didn't. An in-between strategy would be to play cautiously, not risking a lot of chips, saving your stack for The System.

Like the original, the improved System also has you either moving in or folding with every starting hand. But unlike the original System, the hands you move in with will depend on various factors. I have combined those factors into one *key number*. After you calculate that key number you will know which hands to move in with.

Here's how you get that key number. First, divide the total amount of the blinds and antes if they exist into the amount of your stack. If the blinds were $100 and $200, and your stack was $6,000, that would give you a result of 20.

$$20 = \frac{\$6,000}{\$100 + \$200}$$

An important result because it is the odds you are laying to pick up the blinds. $6,000-to-$300 is 20-to-1. *Important exception:* If no one still in the hand has as many chips as you, use the biggest stack among them. That should be obvious, since your risk is no longer your whole stack.

After you have done this division problem, multiply your result by the number of players, including the blinds, yet to act. So if you were one to the right of the button in the previous example, you would multiply by three and get a key number of 60.

$$60 = (3)(20)$$

When there have been no players coming in in front of you, you are done with the calculation. (When someone has already raised in front of you, reraise all in with aces, kings, or ace-king suited. Otherwise fold.) If there are limpers in front of you, multiply the key number by the number of limpers, plus one. In our example, if there were two limpers the key number would now be 180.

$$180 = (3)(60)$$

Here's how to use the key number to decide whether to move in:

- If the key number is 400 or more, move in only with two aces.

- If the key number is between 200 and 400, move in with AA or KK

- If the key number is between 150 and 200, move in with AA, KK, QQ, or AK

- If the key number is between 100 and 150, move in with AA, KK, QQ, JJ, TT, AK, AQ, or KQ

- If the key number is between 80 and 100, move in with any pair, AK, AQ, KQ, any ace suited, and any no gap suited connector down to 54

- If the key number is between 60 and 80, move in with any pair, any ace, KQ, any king suited, and any suited connector with no gap or one gap

- If the key number is between 40 and 60, move in with all of the above, plus any king

- If the key number is between 20 and 40, move in with all of the above, plus any two suited cards

• If the key number is below 20, move in with any two cards.

Let me reiterate that the above guidelines are very far from perfect. A deep analysis, perhaps with the aid of a computer, would result in more precise and accurate criteria. But what I have suggested here ought to do surprisingly well. The biggest problem I can see would occur if you have frequent raisers on your right. In that case, you would need to reraise all in with more than the three hands I recommended.

Let's try a couple of sample hands.

The blinds are $300 and $500. Your stack is $17,000. A player with $12,000 limps in. You are two to the right of the button. The four players yet to act have about ten grand each. You have two sixes. Move in?

Let's calculate the key number. First, notice that the stack size to use is not yours, but rather the largest of the others, $12,000 in this case. Dividing $800 into that number gives us 15.

$$15 = \frac{\$12,000}{\$800}$$

Multiply by four players yet to act gives us 60.

$$60 = (4)(15)$$

Multiplying that by two (due to the one limper) yields 120.

$$120 = (2)(60)$$

That's too high to raise with two sixes since the key number needs to be 100 or less. Notice, however, that if there was one less player behind you, you should raise. Or if your stack was below $10,000. (10,000 divided by 8 = 12.5 x 4 x 2 = 100).

Second example. Nine handed. Blinds $100 and $200. First three fold. You've got $10,000 and some behind you have more. Do you move in with ace-king?

This is simple. Divide 300 into 10,000 to get 33.3. Multiply by the five players yet to act to get a key number of 166.7. Check the key number table. Put the chips in. (But you wouldn't under-the-gun.)

Again, there is no question that this new System could be improved upon. I'd love to see someone do it. But even without those further improvements, I guarantee that it will give tournament pros fits. If you use it, I will be pulling for you.

Folding Aces

I have often heard or read debates about whether or not it can ever be correct to fold two aces before the flop. Some people adamantly say that this play could never be right,[33] and if you are capable of making it, you should never have entered the tournament in the first place. Others claim that situations where such a fold is correct can come up a lot.

This whole debate is rather silly since the chance that you will ever be in a situation where you are dealt two aces and will considering folding is so small. However, just to put this debate to rest, the fact is there are situations where to do anything but fold them would be wrong.

I have great sympathy for those who play in tournaments mainly to win them, without regard to conserving their chances to win a high place below first. However, taking that attitude to an extreme is a bit ridiculous. For instance, suppose you're at the last table at the $10,000 No-Limit Hold 'em World Championship at the World Series of Poker; the blinds are $100,000 and $200,000, and you have $300,000 in tournament chips. The leader has $30 million, and three other players have exactly $10 million. You are in a distant fifth place.

The prize money distribution is:

- First — $15 million
- Second — $10 million
- Third — $7 million
- Fourth — $5 million
- Fifth — $3 million

---

[33] Except in the ultra obvious Super Satellite situation described earlier.

148

At this point an amazing thing happens. One of the players with $10 million moves in and gets called by the other two $10 million stacks. Barring an unlikely tie, you have just made almost $4 million! You were almost certainly going to come in fifth and get $3 million. And now, barring a tie in this three-way pot, you will have $7 million sewn up. What a lucky break! Except for one thing. You look down at your hand and see:

Now what?

The rules of this tournament say that if you go broke at the same time as someone else your prize money depends on how much you started with at the beginning of the hand. So if you play those two aces and lose, you are paid for fifth place only.

If you played the aces and won, you would, again barring ties, find yourself in a three-way situation having $1.2 million in chips against a $30 million dollar stack and a $29.1 million stack. If you stayed out of the hand you would have $300,000 facing two $30 million stacks. Surely I need not bore you with the math that proves that the extra measly $900,000 and the few extra percent chance it gives you of walking away with first or second prize is not worth the significant risk of blowing $4 million when your aces do not stand up against the three other players. That will happen almost half the time.

So to play aces here means you have thrown away $4 million maybe 40 percent of the time, while the other 60 percent of the time you have given yourself, at best, another 10 percent chance to move to second and gain $7 million, and about a 1.2 percent extra chance to go into first and gain $12 million. So 60 percent of the time when your aces win you improve your expectation a little more than $800,000.

$$\$844,000 = (.10)(\$7,000,000) + (.012)(\$12,000,000)$$

and 40 percent of the time you cost yourself $4 million. That's not what you should be trying to achieve and about the only person who should consider playing two aces in this spot is me, since the extra book sales a World Championship would give me might swing the decision to a call — well not really.

Why the
First Day Leader
at the WSOP Never Wins

The $10,000 No-Limit Hold 'em World Championship at the World Series of Poker, which is the final event, lasts at least five days.[34] The game is no-limit hold 'em. After the first day the chip leader typically has about $65,000.[35] I cannot remember a time, although it has probably happened once or twice, where that chip leader has pulled down a major prize. Considering that starting with $65,000 used to give you more than a 10 percent chance to get to the last table, especially in the days when there were less than 300 entrants, it seems odd that these first day leaders don't get there. This might seem doubly true because the chip leader not only has the most chips, but presumably is also playing quite well to accumulate those chips.

But this syndrome is not really odd at all. Remember that the first day of the WSOP used to involve very small blinds culminating late in the day with $100 and $200 blinds and a $50 ante. If you are following the precepts in this book, your first priority is not to go broke. So you would not, for example, risk a large amount of chips on iffy situations. Playing this way normally results in moving your chips up to a maximum of $25,000 or so by the end of the first day.

Often, good players playing this way end up with less than $15,000. There is, of course, always a chance that a perfect hand

---

[34] In 2006 it took a full two weeks.

[35] Today the number is higher since play can last a very long time.

151

will come up that will allow you to win more. But generally, the only way to highly increase your stack is to play in a style that we know is not correct.

Now, let's say the tournament started with 400 players, 200 of whom are using correct tournament precepts, and 200 of whom are taking too many chances (and also may be simply playing badly). At the end of the first day there should be about 230 players left. About 160 of them will come from the tighter group. They will have an average of, let's say $19,000 each. That's $3,040,000.

$$\$3,040,000 = (160)(\$19,000)$$

Only about 70 of the gambling group will be left. They will have an average of about $13,700.

$$\$13,714 = \frac{\$4,000,000 - \$3,040,000}{70}$$

However, their variability is a lot higher. In the first group, most of the players will have between $10,000 and $25,000. In the second group, many will have less than they started with, but a few will have much more.

Usually the chip leader will come from this second group. But this second group is comprised of players who are playing incorrectly. Notice that the 200 original good players who started with $2,000,000 as a whole, have increased their stake to $3,040,000. The other group, as a whole, went from $2,000,000 to $960,000.

$$\$960,000 = \$4,000,000 - \$3,040,000$$

(I use these numbers merely to illustrate a point. In real life the discrepancy is probably not this clear cut.) Nevertheless, because of the volatility of the play of the second group, it is still quite likely that the chip leader will emerge from this group. That being the case, it is not surprising that the chip leader eventually goes down the tubes during the remaining days of the tournament.

Don't get me wrong. Even during the first day of the final tournament of the WSOP you should play selectively aggressively, and certainly not timidly. You merely avoid large pots that are close decisions to ensure survival. It is just that the blinds are too small to allow you to more than double or triple up that first day if you are playing right, unless the cards are completely running over you.

Today, because of the heighten interest in poker, most major tournaments have larger fields than the numbers used in this example. But the precept is still the same. Many of the early leaders will come from the group of players that takes too many chances, and by the end of the tournament, it is unusual for any of these people to make the final table.

Other Topics

Afterthought

While no-limit hold 'em is a great game that certainly can be a terrific test of courage and skill, it does have an "Achilles heel" in a tournament format. Weak players who frequently move in before the flop can negate much of the skill of their better playing opponents and dramatically improve their chances of success.

A few years ago, a totally unknown player finished second in the $10,000 No-Limit Hold 'em World Championship at the World Series of Poker by playing in precisely this fashion. He literally terrorized the field, and several of the well known top players felt at the time that his play was brilliant. In fact, we know that in a sense this really was the case because he had hit upon a simple strategy that made him a very formidable opponent.

The point of this is that our world champion should probably not be determined by a no-limit tournament. Perhaps a tournament consisting of a combination of limit games would be better. But I suspect that tradition will prevail and large buy-in no-limit contests will always be the final event at the major tournaments.

Part Four
Hand Quizzes

Hand Quizzes

Introduction

We now come to what, for many of you, will be the most important part of the book. This is the section which will put the concepts we have learned into action.

When playing poker, it is very important to be able to make your decisions quickly. But they also need to be made accurately. Knowing and understanding theory isn't the same as sitting at the poker table and playing a few hands. Under pressure it is easy to forget and/or confuse concepts and make mistakes. So what can we do to keep this from happening?

Well, one thing is to work through some tournament hands that illustrate many of the ideas we have been talking about. And that's exactly what follows.

Hand Quizzes

1. You are midway through an ace-to-five lowball tournament and have average chips. Everyone folds to you, and you raise with

one to the right of the button. Only the big blind, also with average chips, calls you. He draws two cards. How many should you draw?

> **Answer:** Many of you are probably wondering why the heck this is the first question? We have never even discussed how to play lowball tournaments (because they are so rare) and certainly not discussed how many cards to draw. Plus most of you are probably unfamiliar with this game. But this is a wonderful question to illustrate tournament principles and how they might differ from a side game.
>
> Remember the idea is to maximize your chances of winning pots and to avoid losing bets whenever the alternative (namely gambling) has little or no extra EV. Because of that, the right play in this tournament situation is almost certainly to *stand pat*. That play, though debatable in a side game, is pretty clearcut in a tournament.
>
> In a side game, you would probably draw one (rather than two by the way) to help you win more money after the draw much of the time. If you draw, it is fairly likely you'll make a hand that you can bet and get paid off (by something

157

like a ten or a jack low). But this gamble is not worth it in a tournament.

Keep in mind that the rules of lowball practically force the first player to bet if he makes a seven low or better. Since you stood pat, it is likely that if he comes out betting into you he will have such a hand. Thus, one advantage of standing pat is that you lose less money, compared to drawing, those times he makes a seven. Because if he bets, you fold.

The other advantage is that when he makes a mediocre hand, typically nine through queen, you will always win, since he will not suspect a bluff from your pat hand, but would have, had you drawn. This is especially true in a tournament.

What you give up by standing pat are the calls you would get after the draw when you make a somewhat better hand than he does. Depending on how he plays, that extra call could make drawing slightly better mathematically. But the extra risk you take for that slight gain in EV is probably not worth it in a tournament. So unless you think your opponent has read this book, stand pat.

2. It is somewhere in the middle of a limit hold 'em tournament. No one at your table is on a short stack. Players are playing typically tight. You are under-the-gun with

What do you do?

Answer: The Gap Concept means that in situations like this you almost always fold or raise. It also implies that you should raise with more hands than you would in a side game, including some you would usually fold, because of the much greater chance of stealing the blinds. In spite of all that, those of you who thought you should raise with J♣T♥ are probably wrong. That hand is simply too weak in first position at a full table. The only exception is if you see your opponents are playing ridiculously tight, in which case raising with this hand might be okay.

3. You are at the last table of a seven-card stud tournament. There are five players left. You have slightly less than average chips. You raise with

Another player goes all-in with a nine showing, and a third player, with more chips than you, calls with a ten showing. The nine catches an ace, the ten catches an offsuit four, and you catch a queen. There is no side pot at this point. The ace is all-in, the ten checks; what should you do?

Answer: The idea that you should "check it down" when you are in a three-way pot, where one person is all-in, is usually wrong. If you have a clearly superior hand, you should normally bet, even though that gives the all-in hand a better chance to survive (when others fold). There is however, a situation where you would make this play in a tournament, even though you would not in a regular game. In order for this technique of checking down to be correct, you usually need four things to be the case:

1. You are already in the money or very close to it.

2. You are not a significant favorite over the other player with chips.

3. You are fairly low in chips, and thus are strongly rooting for someone else to go broke.

4. There is a pretty good chance that if you let the third guy in, by checking, he will end up beating the all-in player, while you do not.

   If all these criteria are met, you should, in fact, check on that round. (Although you should not continue to check if succeeding cards turn you into a bigger favorite.) In this particular question all those criteria are in fact met. So, in this precise case, the answer is probably to check.

4. There are two people left; you have $12,000 in chips and your opponent has $10,000. It is no-limit hold 'em. You are up against a world champion. You call a $500 raise before the flop with

The flop is

You are first to act. What do you do?

Answer: Move all-in. If your opponent is aggressive, I will also accept the answer to check raise all-in. What I won't accept is checking and calling, or making a small bet.

Moving all-in with this hand is a fairly routine play if you are betting somewhere around the size of the pot. Betting nine times the size of the pot, as I recommend, is not generally good poker, no matter what your hand. But in this particular case, where you are not likely to outplay this guy, you are better off attempting to let the outcome ride on one hand.

In this example, you are about even money against most one pair hands, and only a slight dog to most better hands. As long as your opponent plays better than you do, getting all the money in on the flop is almost certainly the correct play.

5. It is the middle of an Omaha high-low-split eight-or-better tournament, and no one is on a short stack. Players are playing as they typically do. The under-the-gun player raises, and you are next. You hold

What should you do?

Answer: In a normal game the correct decision is close between calling and folding. In a tournament, reraising is another possibility since it gives you a better than normal chance of being heads-up against the raiser, while having position on him. If you change the ten to a king, I would strongly consider that play since an ace on board is apt to pair both of you. But given the cards I specified, the correct play in a tournament is almost definitely to fold.

6. It is the second level of seven-card stud and no one is on a short stack. Players are playing typically. A deuce brings it in; a jack and a deuce fold; you are next with:

Behind you is a queen, two kings, and a seven, in that order. What should you do?

Answer: This is a good example of a play that probably changes because you are in a tournament. In a side game, you have a close decision, but should probably lean toward folding. In a tournament, you should probably raise. Your chances of stealing the ante are too great. Also your chance of getting reraised by someone without a big pair are reduced.

7. It is late in a limit hold 'em tournament, but still not that near the money tables. You are in the big blind with

everyone folds to the button, who raises, and you have just enough to call that raise. The small blind folds. Do you call?

Answer: You are getting 3½-to-1 odds. Even if he has two over cards or a pair below jacks, 3½-to-1 is much more than enough odds to make the call right. Only if he has a pair of jacks or better would the call be wrong. There is no reason to believe his hand has to be anywhere near that good. Furthermore, survival to pick up a prize should not yet enter your thinking. So your decision should be based purely on your pot odds. (As they would if you were somehow in this situation in a side game.) You have a clear call.

8. There are four tables left. You have an average amount of chips in a limit hold 'em tournament. The last two tables are in the money. Your opponents are playing well. Three of them limp in before the flop. You are on the button with

Should you raise?

Answer: This is a clear raise in a non-tournament game. The question is whether the tournament situation turns this hand into merely a call. Although I think it is close, and I would say otherwise if it was earlier in the tournament, I believe it does. The reason I would not raise is threefold:

1. It is more likely than normal that your hand is not so great in comparison to the other players. They are playing quite tightly, trying to avoid elimination, and some might choose to limp in with hands that dominate or tie the A♥J♥.

2. The extra EV you gain by raising is partially counterbalanced by the fact that making the pot bigger will force you to often lose more money because you have to take one or two extra cards off. For instance, if the flop is

(Giving you two over cards and a three flush) you would often have to at least call a flop bet.

Of course you would win some of those pots, but still, in a tournament small chances of winning big pots, which means large chances of losing some bets is not a good situation, even when the EV is slightly positive. Not raising avoids putting yourself into this situation.

3. Not raising will increase your chances of winning the pot. This occurs even though not raising will sometimes result in one of the blinds, who would have folded a raise, beating you. In spite of that, just calling increases your chances because your opponents are getting lower odds when you, or someone else, bets into them later on.

They are, therefore, more apt to fold a hand that might have drawn out on you. Also, by not raising, you are more likely to be bet into when an ace or jack flops, which allows you to thin the field by raising now.

Of course, the downside of making this play to increase your chances of winning the pot, is that the pots you win will be smaller. However, late in the tournament, when your chip stack is not high enough to ensure getting into the money, I believe the upside outweighs the downside, although again I think it is close. (It is so close that I am sure that you should raise if your hand was ace-king suited and probably ace-queen suited.)

9. You are at the last table with seven players left in a seven-card stud tournament. A 2♣ brings it in, and an 8♥ raises. You're next and have

The player on your immediate left does not have enough chips to play a hand to the river. He is showing a T♦. Behind him is a 4♣, Q♠, and J♠. You are in fifth place, chip wise. Do you call or reraise?

Answer: In side games, it is reasonable to slowplay small rolled up hands, even when one of your trip cards is out. In a tournament, it is less reasonable because, with close decisions, it is usually better to maximize your chances of winning the pot. This is especially true at the last table.

However, this particular situation is different. You have a chance to bust the short stack, which is particularly good for you since you are on low chips yourself. If you just call, the short stack will almost certainly play a pair of tens and may even play three high cards such as

since the raiser had an eight showing. If you reraise, however, he will certainly fold those hands, not only because of the strength that you showed, but also because of the two overcards behind him. Plus, he would see an opportunity to sit back and root for you to dissipate your chips. So in this specific situation, I believe you should deviate from the normally correct tournament strategy of reraising and merely call.

10. It is the last table of a limit hold 'em tournament. The blinds are $500 and $1,000. You have $2,000 left and have to put in the big blind, leaving you with $1,000. The two players on your left both have $1,500 in front of them. The other three players have more than $30,000 each. Everyone folds to the button who raises to $2,000. The small blind folds. You have

Should you call?

Answer: Even though you know the button will raise with almost anything, which means your K♠T♠ will win more than half the time, this is an extraordinary circumstance. If there is a big money jump between fourth, fifth, and sixth place, you should probably throw your hand away and the next hand as well. There is an excellent chance that this strategy will move you into fifth place and a good chance it will move you all the way into fourth place. That is because the two players on your left must go all-in with anything before you have to put your last $500 in. Notice also, if you did play and win, you are still far below the third place player. Thus you should fold K♠T♠ and similar hands in this situation.

I would not take this to an extreme, however. With two aces, your chances of winning are so great, I believe you should call and take the risk of going broke. That is because winning here brings you up to $4,500 which gives you an even better chance of winning at least fourth place and some small chance of finishing higher.

11. Seven-card stud. Middle of the tournament. No one is on a short stack. A 2♠ brings it in. A 7♥ folds. And you are next with

Behind you in order are the 6♣, 5♣, Q♦, and J♥. Should you call, raise, or fold?

Answer: This is a perfect example of a situation where the fact that you are in a tournament will probably change your strategy. In a side game, this hand is normally not quite worth playing. However, in a tournament, against players who are playing typically, you have a raising hand. That is because small pairs and any three card straights will now probably fold, even though they might have called in a side game.

This answer is, of course, a generic one. If for some reason you find that players are playing differently from how typical tournament players play, you will adjust accordingly. But as a general principle, in seven-card stud tournaments, you should raise with all but your worst hands when no one else is yet in, and you have the (unduplicated) highest card showing.

12. There are two tables left in a limit hold 'em tournament with six players at each table. Most of the money goes to the last nine at the final table. The blinds are $200 and $400. You have $3,000, and it is less than average. The two players in the blinds have about $1,200 each. Everyone folds to you on the button, and you have

What should you do?

Answer: Even though you are in jeopardy of not making the last table, not raising in this situation would be wrong if the players in the blinds are typical. There is simply too great a chance that you will steal those blinds.

I say this because of the precise size of their stacks. If they had either more or less, they would call you fairly liberally. (With more, because there is no reason not to play normal poker strategy, and with less, because they can't wait any longer.) But with these size stacks, they will probably elect to throw away marginal hands in the hopes that something better will come along or that they can sneak into the last table with their remaining chips.

You should take advantage of that. Keep in mind that you will still have $2,200 if your raise gets called and you give up. That often will still be enough to make the last table.

I might have answered this question differently if your stack had been significantly smaller. It is also not irrelevant that your hand included a king. You just might hit that king and bust one of the blinds.

13. It is the last table. You are the chip leader in a limit hold 'em tournament. You raise with

and get one call behind you by a player who is now all-in. You also get calls from the two blinds. There is no side pot. The flop comes

Both blinds check. Should you bet?

Answer: If you do not bet, the player who is all-in is in big trouble. More so if you check again on fourth street. That is why it is common practice for players to have sort of a gentleman's agreement to check to each other any hands that are not very strong when there is a player who is all-in. This is doubly true when there is no side pot. By playing this way, everyone increases their chances of moving up one place.

But besides possibly being ethically wrong, that strategy is also strategically wrong when you have a lot of chips. It will almost never matter to you whether the next person who goes broke is the all-in guy or somebody else. It only significantly matters to those who are in danger of going broke next if the all-in guy doesn't. In this particular situation, betting the flop with ace-king will get the blinds to fold more than they normally would. Not only because they are less apt to gamble with higher prizes coming up, but also (maybe) because they don't think that you would violate this supposed well known principle of checking mediocre hands down when someone is all-in. So go ahead and bet. Sure it might allow the all-in player to win a pot and survive where he might otherwise not. So what? It also might win you a pot with no further risk (since you get your last bet back when the blinds fold).

14. In the middle of a seven-card stud tournament, no one is short stacked at your table, you have called a raise on third street with

and one other spade is out. You have two opponents. On fourth street you catch the K♦ and there is a bet and a call. Should you call?

> **Answer:** This is probably an example of a situation in which you would switch your play between a side game and a tournament. It is often marginally correct in a side game to take one more card off when you break off a fairly live three flush on fourth street, especially if you catch a big card. However, if you are one of the better players, in a tournament you should usually fold in this same situation.
>
> The problem with this particular hand is that taking a card off is not only risking one bet that will usually be lost, but that it will often risk additional bets that also could be lost. You don't need to get involved in these types of close gambling situations if you are a good tournament player.

15. It is the middle of an Omaha high-low-split eight-or-better tournament. No one is on a short stack. Two players have folded. You have

What do you do?

> **Answer:** Unlike hold 'em, it is often right, playing Omaha high-low-split eight-or-better, to merely limp in, even when no one else has limped in front of you. This is because there are more hands in Omaha that crave multiple opponents behind them, and smaller chances to win the whole pot with a raise before the flop. The above hand is a good example of

one, that in early position, in a ring game is usually best to just call with. However, this would not normally be the case in a tournament. Because of the way players typically tighten up in the face of a raise while playing tournaments, it means that raising with this hand is more likely to instantly win the blinds. Yet merely limping is not as apt to result in a multiway pot. Thus you should probably raise.

16. Three players have folded; no one is short stacked, and you have

in a limit hold 'em tournament. Call, raise, or fold?

Answer: Notice that I did not mention how far along you are in the tournament because it doesn't matter. If opponents are playing the way they typically do, the Gap Concept applies perfectly here and you must raise.

There are side games where calling would be better because you will entice many to limp behind you. There are also side games where folding should be considered because a raise will not get out hands like ace-jack, king-ten, or queen-jack. But neither of these types of games is likely to be what you are facing in a tournament.

A limp will not entice other limps, but a raise will get out lots of hands that you want out, and may even steal the blinds. As a general rule, once a few players have folded, you should never limp before the flop in a limit hold 'em tournament, and your raising hands don't have to be that great.

17. There are four tables left in a no-limit hold 'em tournament. Prizes are paid to the last two tables. The blinds are $100 and $200. You have $4,200, which is slightly less than average, and you are holding

in the big blind. All fold to the button, who puts in $800 and has $6,000 left. The small blind folds. What should you do?

Answer: There are three possible reasons not to move all-in. One would be that your opponent is very tight and will thus have the dreaded aces or kings a significant portion of the time. Another reason would be that your opponent plays badly from the flop on allowing you to extract extra money when an ace or a king hits and save money when you don't have the best hand. A third reason would be that you are far superior to most of the players in this tournament and would hate to risk going broke with this non-paired hand.

These three reasons are legitimate, but almost always not good enough given your opponent raised first in on the button. I would still move in here almost every time, and so, probably, should you.

18. It is the middle of a limit hold 'em tournament. No one is on a short stack. Five players fold before the flop; the next player (a very good tournament player) raises. You have

Answer: Once this many players fold, it is almost never correct to flat call a raiser unless you are in the big blind. This is even more true in a tournament than in a side game. Because players tend to play a little bit tighter, however, your reraising hands need to be a bit better, with one important exception. That is when the original raiser is familiar with the Gap Concept. (Most of the best players were, even before I wrote this book.) When such a player raises with no one else in yet, his hands will, on average, be a little bit worse than they would be in a side game. Thus, your reraising hands can be a bit worse too. Not only because of his hand, but because the players behind you will throw all but the very best hands away for three bets cold. Clearly then, you should reraise with your two jacks in this situation. (However, against a less expert-type player, it might be right to fold.)

19. It is a seven-card stud tournament, midway through the levels. There are no short stacks. A 2♥ brings it in. Three players fold, and a good tournament player, showing an A♠, raises. Two more fold, and you have

Your cards are live. What should you do?

Answer: This question is similar to the one preceding it. The player with the A♠ is very likely not to have aces. However, unlike hold 'em, reraising, especially in a tournament, may not be a good idea.

There are two differences between this and the previous hold 'em example. One is that a pair of jacks is less likely to be the best hand in stud, especially when it is facing an open ace. The second reason is that the original raiser has a much better idea of what you have, and can take advantage of it. In the hold 'em example, the first raiser has to be scared that your hand is even better than two jacks. Not nearly as much so in stud. Still, J♦T♦J♣ is far too good a hand to throw away, even in a tournament. That's probably true even if you were sure you were facing two aces. So you must at least call.

Reraising however, while not a terrible play, opens yourself up to his reraising, which in turn will make the pot so big that you will usually have to play the hand all the way to the river. This is not the kind of situation you want to be in when you are one of the best players in the tournament, i.e. playing a big pot as a probable underdog.

Therefore, I believe that the right answer to this question is to merely call unless your opponent will raise with practically any three cards. Unlike most of the other questions, I do believe the answer is close. But I included it in order to illustrate this tournament principle that applies specifically to stud.

20. Back to limit hold 'em. Again, a mid-level situation with no short stacks. Four players limp, including the small blind. You check in the big blind with

The flop is

You check. Someone bets and gets two calls. What should you do?

Answer: In a side game, I would usually just call here. In a tournament, I would always just call. The plan is to root for a blank, and go for a check raise on fourth street. When your hand holds up and you play it that way, you usually win at least as much as you would have had you check raised the flop. But that is only part of the reason you don't raise the flop. The bigger reason, which takes on more importance in a tournament, is that you can save money when a bad card comes off. The worst card is probably an eight; other bad cards are queen, jack, nine, and seven. When they come off you should check again, and be prepared to fold if it is a cold raise to you. The general principle here is that the often used (by experts) tactic of waiting until fourth street to see if a bad card comes off, is even more indicated in limit hold'em tournaments.

Note: In this question I did not have you coming right out betting on the flop because I wanted to make a point. Do not infer that I believe checking the flop is necessarily always the right play.

21. Getting back to stud, that same hand where the A♠ raised and you flat called with the J♣ showing and a J♦T♦ in the hole. On fourth street he catches an offsuit 7♥, and you catch a T♥. He bets. You are now almost sure he has aces, given that bet. You just call. On fifth street you catch a 7♣ which is the same suit as your upcard. He catches a 5♦ and bets again. What should you do?

Answer: In our book, *Seven-Card Stud for Advanced Players,* we address the situation where you have two hidden pair on fifth street and are facing a bet from an obvious big pair (or possibly better hand). We point out that raising here is probably not as good an idea as waiting until the next card, in order to see whether he pairs his board. If he does, you save money. And if he doesn't, you get your raise in on sixth street.

However, the problem with waiting is that you will sometimes catch a card on sixth street that keeps him from betting into you. When there may be many such cards it is usually right to make the fifth street raise. But because this is a close decision, I believe the proper strategy in most tournament situations is to wait. This is yet another example of opting for the less volatile play when the two alternatives are close, and it is similar to the hold'em example above. As I've been emphasizing throughout this book, if you are one of the best players in the tournament, you should avoid committing excess chips early in a hand on close decisions, not only because you are gambling with those chips, but also because your making the pot bigger may force you to gamble further with even more chips.

22. Seven-card stud, midway through the tournament. The 2♣ brings it in. The J♠ raises. Three other unduplicated cards below a jack call, including a couple of short stacks. You are last with

What do you do?

Answer: I threw this question in to keep anyone from trying to guess my answers merely because I asked the question. That is a natural inclination when you take a quiz, but I don't want you doing that. Just answer these questions as if they came up while you were playing. Don't try to figure out what tricky reason I may have had to ask them. Here you raise of course.

23. You are down to five players in a seven-card stud tournament. Everyone has approximately the same number of chips and cannot go broke on one hand. The 2♣ brings it in. The J♠ raises. You are next with

What do you do?

Answer: In a tournament it is important to win the pots you play. It is doubly important when you are at the last table. Slowplaying big hands to suck other people in is not right nearly as often as it would be in a side game. Getting heads-up with the best hand is something you should usually be striving for.

However, all of these principles assume that you are choosing between two fairly close plays. This one is not close. With three rolled up aces you give up way too much when you knock everyone out. Yes, a reraise will increase your chances of winning the pot. But your chances are already so high that you must try to win an even bigger pot here.

Had your three-of-a-kind been smaller than some of the upcards, the right play would probably reverse, and you should reraise, even though you might not in a side game. But it would be a sin not to try to get as much as you could out of these three bullets.

24. In the middle of a limit hold 'em tournament you are in the big blind, with

Four players limp. The flop is

Everyone checks. The turn is the 9♥. Everyone checks. The last card is the J♠. What do you do?

> **Answer:** In the text I point out a similar situation where I recommend bluffing on the river after everyone has checked twice. But this is different. Here the cards are getting higher, not lower, and are thus much more likely to have hit someone. You would be getting less than 3-to-1 on your bluff, and I don't believe it is worth trying.

25. It is the first hour of the $10,000 No-Limit Hold 'em World Championship at the World Series of Poker. The blinds are $25 and $50. The first player raises to $300. The second player calls. Two more players call behind him. You make it $2,000 to go with

The initial raiser folds. The first caller folds. The second caller moves in $10,000. You have never seen him before. The other caller folds as well. Should you call?

Answer: I bring up this question because I have seen this type of situation occur no less than three times. In all three cases the kings called. In all three cases those with the kings needed to have their heads examined. Seriously, a call in this spot is insane. I mean, what do they think that guy had? Sure he played the hand oddly. You would have expected him to raise the first time around if he had aces. But that still does not change anything. He has aces. (Or just maybe kings. But even if he will play two kings this way you still can't call since there is only one combination of kings he could have versus six combinations of aces. At this point you would be getting odds of approximately 8-to-5 if you called. Assuming this occurred 70 times, and he had aces 60 times, and kings 10 times, the results would be: Ten times you would split the pot and make about $2,500 compared to folding, eleven times you would make about $13,500 compared to folding, and 49 times you would lose $8,000, plus go broke. So you can see that even if he might have kings, calling is horrible.)

Why am I so sure he has aces or just maybe kings? Put yourself in his shoes. He has to seriously worry that you have a pair of aces. You, after all, put in that big reraise against all those other players. Is he going to jeopardize all of his chips in the hopes you don't? Does it make any sense that he would do this with a pair of queens? You do sometimes see this play with ace-king suited. But not when it costs so much, and not when it is so likely that he is facing aces or kings. (And though I didn't point it out in the first edition, it *still* would be wrong to call even if he could have ace-king suited. Do you see why?)

Those three players who made this call with the two kings were all considered good players. But I lost a little respect for each of them. They were not able to adjust to a unique situation. All they knew was that their hand was two kings, a ridiculous hand to fold pre-flop in normal situations, and that the other player's play did not coincide with the way two aces would normally be played. But they did not have the skill to realize that those factors were irrelevant. As a secondary error, they did not understand that even if it was close, they should not be moving all their chips in this early in a tournament since all three were in the top 10 percent of all players skill wise.

I should point out that the reason this fold is so clear cut is that the initial blinds were so small compared to the size of the stacks. That ratio is not true to this degree in just about any other poker tournament. And as the stacks shrink compared to the blinds, it will never be as undebatable to fold two kings before the flop as it is here.

26. It is the beginning of a limit hold 'em tournament. Four people limp in. And you have

on the button. What should you do?

Answer: Raise. This is the right way to play in a side game. In a tournament, you would seriously consider flat calling. You don't want to risk an extra bet with a very slight edge, and more importantly, you don't want to increase the size of the pot to the point where you will have to risk even more chips in a situation where you will probably not win the pot. Except, this is the first level. Because of that, tournament preservation strategies don't matter much. You are playing well within your bankroll. So if a play is even slightly right to do, you should do it.

A secondary advantage is that it will create the impression that you are not playing an especially tight tournament strategy, even though you, in fact, will be playing tightly as soon as the stakes are raised. Thus, the play is especially advantageous when your table will not be broken up for awhile.

27. It is the middle of a no-limit hold 'em tournament. None of the relevant players are short stacked. The blinds are $25 and $50, and you have $5,000 in front of you. Two people limp in. You raise $200 with

The blinds fold and the limpers call. The flop is

Both players check. You bet $600. They both call. The next card is the 2♥. They both check. How much should you bet?

Answer: The answer to this question happens to be the same for both tournaments and side games. However, to play it incorrectly is even worse in a tournament. The answer is well known to good no-limit players, but may not be to you if your only no-limit experience is tournaments. Anyway, the amount you bet is $0. Had the fourth card not been a heart, it may or may not have been right to bet this hand, depending on how likely you think you are being trapped. But when the heart comes, it is usually very wrong to bet.

The principle is one that was mentioned in the text. You should not bet in last position, or raise another bettor, if you will hate him raising back. This concept rarely relates to limit poker because there are not many times when you would truly hate someone raising you. The worst that happens is that you lose an extra bet. But in no-limit, a raise can be large enough where you have to throw your hand away, even though your chances of winning are significant. In this particular situation, if you bet, say $1,500, and one of the other two players check raised all-in, you are in major trouble. Almost certainly you are beat.

The problem is that you have a draw to the nuts, but not the pot odds to call. (Actually, even if you did have good enough pot odds you're still in major trouble because you are now forced to call with a hand that will probably lose.) Thus, in situations like this, you should almost always check because you would hate to see a raise.

Without the four hearts, you could bet, because a raise means you are probably drawing dead. So folding does not hurt you. You also can bet if your hand is so good that you welcome the raise. But neither of those situations exist here. Thus you take a free card.[36]

28. The game is limit hold 'em. The stakes are $100-$200 with a $50 and $100 blind. All fold to the button who makes it $200.

---

[36] Keep in mind that this play assumes you are in last position. If you are not, the right answer is not as clear because you cannot prevent further betting with a check. So you might want to bet yourself. But there is still a good reason to check. It is that this allows you to have high implied odds if you merely call the bet behind you.

The small blind folds. You started this hand with $300 and have $200 after putting in the blind. Your hand is

Should you call, reraise all-in, or fold?

Answer: Before answering this question, we do have to agree on some assumptions — assumptions that would accurately describe the vast majority of opponents. Number one is that they will raise with a lot of hands. That is a standard play in this spot. Second, we assume that a reraise before the flop by you will always be called. Obviously. He's getting $550-to-$100 odds on that all-in reraise. Third we assume that if you call before the flop, and check on the flop, he will usually bet. I am sure you agree that almost all opponents will play this way. So let's start the analysis.

First, let's see if you should possibly throw the A♣2♦ away. You are getting 3½-to-1 on his raise which would make this an easy call if you were all in. The problem is that extra $100 in your stack. Might that change things?

If you shove it in before the flop, the real odds you are getting are no longer $350-to-$100. They have gone down to $450-to-$200 or 2½-to-1. Is it worth taking those odds with A♣2♦?

Well, of course it is. If he would raise with anything, your hand would actually be a slight favorite. But even if he was throwing bad hands away, there is no way his remaining hands would beat you anywhere near the 69 percent or so needed to make it right to fold.

This means that we have established that folding cannot be right. We have also showed that reraising shows a profit (if the big blind is counted as no longer yours). That beats folding and breaking even.

In fact, I believe most players would reraise in this spot. But there are alternatives. You could merely call before the flop. And then depending on what came, you could bet, check and call, or check and fold. Let's look at these alternatives.

First, notice that, if you always called before the flop, and then check and called on the flop, you would essentially be in the same position as you would have been had you raised before the flop. Given the fact that your check will almost always elicit a bet, playing that way results in a showdown for the $650 pot. Just like your reraise would. So this strategy gains nothing over the all-in raise.

But what about checking and sometimes folding? Oh yeah? When would you do that? You would be getting $550-to-$100 on his flop bet and you have an ace. Between the times you catch an ace and the times ace high wins unimproved, your chances would always total more than the necessary 15 percent to win the pot.

So checking and folding is out. And checking and always calling is no better than reraising pre-flop. What about calling before the flop and betting out on the flop? The problem of course with this play is that it allows your opponent to save a bet when he flops nothing. Moving in before the flop prevents this. But wait. What odds is he getting on your flop bet? Again it is $550-to-$100. Suppose the flop is

and he has

Your bet has probably caused him to fold a hand with six outs! He is less than a 5½-to-1 dog so he costs himself money by folding. Money (actually EV) that you gained. Had you reraised pre-flop you would have won an extra $100 most of the time to be sure. But that isn't enough to make up for the risk of losing the pot on the turn or the river.

It is true that there are not too many flops that your bet will make him "incorrectly" fold. But so what? It is simply getting extra equity with everything else being equal. Unless you flop aces or better, your bet on the flop will always be one that you want him not to call (except for some of the rare times he has a deuce).

And what about those times you do flop aces? Check it, of course. He will probably bet it for you even with hands that he would have folded had you bet.

Note: I originally wrote about this hand in a magazine article. A reader quickly dubbed my suggested play the "stop and go play." The no-limit version is discussed in "The Stop 'n Go Play" starting on page 228 in "Part Five: Additional No-Limit Concepts."

29. The following question applies to any stage of the tournament. You have been betting all the way against one player, who you think is on a draw. On the river you check, and he bets. Should you tend to call him with hands that cannot beat his draw if he makes it?

> **Answer:** Although your opponents in tournaments will typically be more cautious than usual, this situation, in my experience, is an exception. I believe players in tournaments will bluff in this spot at least as often as they would in a side game. Of course, every player has to be evaluated individually. However, if this is a player you would call in this spot in a side game, I would definitely call him here.

30. As in the previous question, this situation can occur at any level of the tournament. Again you are betting all the way. But this time you think that your reasonably good hand is also worth betting on the river. When you bet, he raises. His raise represents a hand better than yours. So you can only beat a bluff. Should you tend to call?

> **Answer:** In the answer to the previous question I stated that in my experience tournament players are just as likely to make a bluffing bet on the end as they would in a side game. However, I believe a bluffing *raise* is a different story. Players who are trying to conserve chips are not anxious to throw away two precious big bets. So unless you have good reason to think otherwise about this player, I would tend to believe his raise even more in a tournament than I would in a side game. And, in spite of the pot odds, I would seriously consider folding.

31. The game is seven-card stud. The stakes have reached $150-$300, with a $25 ante and a $50 bring-in. Your table is eight handed. You are down to your last $75, $25 of which you

have antied. The player on your right brings it in with the 2♣.
Your hand is the

Behind you are no tens or deuces, but there is an ace and a
queen. Should you play?

Answer: It is almost equivalent to the hold 'em situation in
which there are two more hands before it gets to your blind.
If you don't play now, you will certainly have to play one of
the next two hands. (The difference is that if you play now,
and win, you will win more than if you wait until the bitter
end, because your antes are dissipating.)

We learned in the text that, with one hand to go before
your last hand, you should elect to play hands that are
somewhat better than the average hand you would get if you
waited until the end. With two hands to go you should play
hands that are even better still, though not as good as what
you would need under normal circumstances.

I do not believe that your pair of deuces is good enough
to meet this criterion. I am almost positive that you are better
off waiting, even though a pair only comes along about one
in six times. The problem is that this pair is so small (and
dead). So I think you should fold. However, it is close. And
I would change my answer if any of the following five things
were different:

1. Your pair was slightly higher.

2. There was no other deuce showing.

3. Your kicker was higher than any of the other upcards.

4. Some players had already folded. Or,

5. There was only one hand, rather than two hands to go before you were forced all in.

Again, if any one of these five things were true, I believe that would be enough to make you play.

32. In the middle of an Omaha high-low-split eight-or-better tournament, you have an average number of chips. You have the button. Your hand is

Before the flop the under-the-gun player raised and got five calls, including you. (Reraising is okay too.) The blinds have folded. The flop is

The under-the-gun player bets, the next player raises, and everyone calls. So what should you do?

Answer: This is not a case where tournament considerations can override your best play. Your hand is just too good.

Furthermore, playing cautiously will not allow you to escape this hand before the river as it might in some other spots. You should reraise here. Period.

33. It is the middle of a limit hold 'em tournament. No one is on a short stack. Three people limp in, and you call in the small blind with

The flop is

Should you come out betting?

Answer: Almost definitely. Semi-bluffs on the flop in limit hold 'em would tend to work even better in a tournament than in a side game. By that I mean that one of the two aspects of a semi-bluff, namely the chance of winning immediately, usually increases in a tournament. The fact that an ace is on board also probably helps your chances of stealing the pot, since other players fear that ace if they don't have one themselves.

With a gut shot straight draw and a back door flush draw you will make a pat hand about one-fourth of the time you are played with. If you don't bet, you often would have to call if someone else did (or fold the hand you wish you could play). So it is usually better to bet yourself and give yourself the chance to win it right there. Another reason to bet is that hands like jack-ten will fold, which increases your chances of winning if you get called by something like a pair of eights.

34. Again, it is limit hold 'em. An early position player raises and gets three calls. The small blind folds. You call from the big blind with

The flop comes

Should you bet?

Answer: Again, yes. There is a much smaller chance you will win the pot immediately, but it doesn't matter. It is still probably worth doing. The key here, though, is that an ace fell. By betting into everyone you will often make the raiser fold as good as a pair of kings. If you can do that, you might well win the pot instantly. Plus, a call from the other players can come with hands that you can beat if you catch as little as a ten or a nine. And as before, your bet will fold hands like king-ten or jack-nine.

The only real risk in betting is that you will be raised, and then go on and lose the pot. EV-wise that possibly costs you a fraction of a small bet. Therefore, if your bet increases your chances of winning the whole pot just slightly, that should more than make up that fraction of a bet.

35. It is limit hold 'em, and again you have the T♦9♦ in the big blind against the same raiser and callers as the previous quiz hand. The flop is

Should you bet?

Answer: Again, the answer is yes. In tournaments, the raiser on your left will often fold a pocket pair between nines and aces. Once you get by him you may win immediately. Even when you don't, you probably have five outs, plus a back door flush draw. Some of the times you don't win immediately, you are merely called by a hand that would have bet had you checked. So the bet cost you no more than a check and call would have. The fact that you might be raised is not a good enough reason, in most cases, to opt for a check with your hand.

One important thing to realize about this hand and the two above it is that my admonition to avoid close gambles does not apply to those times that a gamble can increase your chances of winning the pot. Semi-bluffs early on should be made at least as often in tournaments as in side games.

36. It is a no-limit hold 'em tournament. There are 14 players left. The serious prize money starts being awarded to the nine players at the last table. The blinds are $100 and $200. The total amount of chips is $140,000. You have $15,000 in front of you. Both the small and the big blind have $3,400 in front of them. No one is in and you are on the button, and hold

What should you do?

Answer: Raise to about $900. I pick this number for a good reason. It needs to be high enough so that the two short stacks in the blind will be very reluctant to play unless they have a hand that is worth moving in before the flop. This is a very important concept. Had you raised a lesser amount, say to $600, they might call with hands like

or

with the intention of folding if they did not like the flop. Once you raise to $900 or $1,000, however, you have cut their implied odds and made them risk more money than they want to, (especially under the tournament circumstances), as far as flat calling is concerned. Thus, your raise has pretty much forced them to either fold or move all in.

A typical player in this spot will, in my experience, throw away about 90 percent of his hands. That means you will get away with your bluff about 80 percent of the time. Risking $900 to win the $300 blinds ought to be profitable.

Notice, however, that a somewhat bigger opening bet on your part is wrong. If you open for $1,200, you would practically guarantee that you would either steal the blinds or get moved in on. But those hands that would move in on you figure to remain the same, whether you bet $900 or $1,200. So the extra $300 that you risked, got you nothing in return.

I hope I don't have to spell out the fact that if you are reraised, you fold. Notice, by the way, that the fact you had J♣7♥ was almost inconsequential. You will rarely see any flops, so you could have just as easily made this play with seven-deuce. And given the expected proclivities of the two players in the blind who are trying hard to make the last table, you should in fact play seven-deuce that way as well.

37. It is a no-limit hold 'em tournament with several tables left. When all the cards are out there is $1,800 in the pot. Three hearts are on board, but no pair, and your opponent checks to you. You have the nut flush. He has $1,200 in front of him and you have more. How much should you bet?

Answer: The answer obviously depends to some degree on how the hand was played and who your opponent is. But I am trying to illustrate a specific concept with this question. Remember that one of the keys to good tournament play is to take advantage of the fact that your opponents don't want to go broke. (We assume there are no rebuys available.) That fact allows us to steal pots we might not ordinarily steal. And in fact, in this situation, it might be right to move in if you had only the ace of the suit in question, but no flush.

However, you do have the flush, so the syndrome is reversed. We have to assume that this guy is less likely than normal to call an all in bet. $1,200 is not normally an out of line size bet given the size of the pot, but I don't believe it is the right bet in this spot. You need to give him hope to come back in case he loses. You should probably make a bet that will leave him with some chips — somewhere between $500 and $800.

38. It is the middle of a limit hold 'em tournament. No one is on a short stack. A player raises under-the-gun. All fold to you. You have

in the big blind. Should you call?

Answer: Absolutely not. This is a simple example where the right play is clearly different in a tournament than in a side game. 90 percent of tournament players need a better hand than usual to raise under-the-gun. Furthermore, they will play those hands cautiously. That means that if they have a pocket pair and an ace flops, you will win less than you would in a side game. Meanwhile your chances of flopping a ten and having it be a loser are greater than normal, as is your chance of flopping an ace and having it be a loser. Add all of that to the fact that you are trying to avoid close gambles, and you have a clear cut fold. In fact, I almost asked this question with you having ace-jack, rather than ace-ten. That would be closer, but still would almost certainly be a hand to fold.

39. It is the middle of a no-limit hold 'em tournament. The blinds are $100 and $200. Four people fold to a player who makes it $800 to go, and has $10,000 left. You know that he is aware of the Gap Concept. No one calls until it gets to you. You have

on the button and $4,000 in your stack. What should you do?

Answer: I believe this is one of those times you should move all in. Had his raise been larger, there would be no question about it.

We know he is raising with a lot of hands. So we cannot fold. If he had opened for, say, $1,500, it would be quite wrong to flat call. The flop might be a tough one to play, so you would rather be all in, or better yet, have him fold immediately.

However, when he raises to only $800, many players would be inclined to merely call and see what comes. That might very well allow them to conserve $3,200 in chips. I don't agree.

Again, I want to reemphasize that my admonition against close gambles that might make you broke does not apply to times that a close gamble can win you the pot without a fight. If you move in here, he will fold a large percentage of his hands. Those times he doesn't fold, you will win somewhat less than half the time. But all told, you should still show a nice profit.

Had you had, say, $7,000 in front of you, rather than $4,000, the right play would have more likely been to simply call. Moving in $7,000 is a lot more risk for essentially the same reward. And raising only $4,000 is really the same as raising $7,000, since if he did play, he would undoubtedly move you the rest of the way in. But when you have $4,000, your raise is exactly within the range that I recommend in the text, somewhere between two to fives times the size of the pot.

40. You are down to three players. The leader has $25,000 in chips, you have $15,000 and the other player has $5,000. The prize money is $10,000 for first, $5,000 for second, and $3,000 for third. The other two players are good friends and would rather not play against each other. They point out that you are exactly in the middle between first and third, and ought to finish second, so that $5,000 is what they offer you to end the tournament. Your buddy, meanwhile, points out that if all three of the players had $15,000, they each would average a third of the total or $6,000. Since you do in fact have a third of the money, he says $6,000 would be the fair settlement. Who is right?

Answer: You ought to win this tournament one out of three times. When you don't win, you will probably be against the short stack (for second place) that you now have a 3-to-1 chip lead over. A good estimate of your possible results would be that in 12 such similar situations you would win four, and of the remaining eight, come in second, six times. Thus, four times you would make $10,000, six times you would make $5,000 and two times you would make $3,000. That adds up to $76,000 over 12 tournaments, or an average of $6,333.

$$\$6,333 = \frac{(4)(\$10,000) + (6)(\$5,000) + (2)(\$3,000)}{12}$$

That is quite a bit more than the $5,000 they offered you. It is not surprising.

What might be surprising, however, is that even your buddy's recommendation was too small. The reason has to do with the fact that you have a better chance of playing for the top prize than you would if you all started out equally. To make this clear, suppose the leader had $29,000, while the other guy had $1,000 and you still had $15,000. You still have a one-third chance of winning, but your chances of coming in third have gone down further still.

Again, I want to say that the mathematical method that was used in this problem is not perfectly accurate, but it is close enough.

41. It is somewhere toward the end of a seven-card stud tournament. No one at your table is on a short stack. A 2♦ brings it in. A couple of small cards fold; and a player with a Q♠ showing, raises. This player is very familiar with the Gap Concept. Behind him is your 7♥, followed by the J♠ and a 9♣. You have

Should you call, reraise or fold?

Answer: This is unquestionably a reraising situation. There is a very good chance that the queen has a worse hand than you. And if it is in fact two queens you are facing, you have a king kicker, which makes you only a small underdog if the hand is played heads up. Also, a key point is that your reraise will almost certainly result in a heads up pot, even if there is a pair of jacks or nines behind you. No way will typical players call with those hands, especially in a tournament, since they not only fear your reraise, but also fear the player who made the original raise with the queen.

If instead there had been an ace showing behind you, your reraise would have been much more debatable. Not only because the ace could have aces, but also because the queen would less likely be semi-bluffing with a weak hand.

42. It is the last table of a no-limit hold 'em tournament. The blinds are $500 and $1,000, and there is a $200 ante. The average stack is $30,000. You have $10,000, which is the shortest stack. The next shortest is $13,000. You are dealt

under-the-gun. What should you do?

Answer: This is a close decision between all three alternatives. Actually there are four alternatives because if you choose to raise you might raise either a small or large amount. And in fact, if you had lots of money in front of you, you might well make it $3,000 or $4,000 to go. The problem with this play when you only have $10,000 total is that you cannot fold if you are reraised.

Therefore, if you do opt to raise, you might as well move in right from the beginning. That play has the advantage of getting some hands out that you want out. For instance, a pair of nines or king-queen suited is apt to fold to the bigger raise, but not the smaller one.

What about just calling? That is a definite alternative when there are few players raising before the flop, especially when you have a lot of chips in front of you. The idea would be to call, hope no one else raises, and enjoy high implied odds. With only $10,000 in front of you, however, you cannot get great implied odds.

It still might be worth a mere call if you're putting a lot of emphasis on moving up the prize ladder, but again, only if there are few players who are pre-flop raising. Given you are at the last table at this tournament, that is not likely to be the case.

Since it is likely that a limp on your part will be raised, might that indicate that it is better to simply throw the hand away? That would depend on the chip and the prize situation. If there is a reasonable chance that players will be going broke before you have anted off your money, you may very well want to fold here. Then again, it would probably be better, even in this situation, to limp for $1,000, hope you won't be raised, but fold if you are.

But in this specific case you have the lowest stack and can expect the slightly bigger stacks to wait you out. With that $3,000 or so sitting in the pot, I believe the best play is to just move in. You could easily win it right there. And even when you are called you will sometimes have the best hand.

I would change my answer to limping and then folding to a raise if there was no ante or if the other short stacks were gambling it up. But in the typical scenario I'd push in my $10,000.

43. It is the middle of a limit hold 'em tournament. A player in middle position raises. You are the only caller with

in the big blind. The flop is

How should you play the flop and fourth street?

Answer: Check raise on the flop, and then bet all the way. This is often the right way to play in a side game as well, but it is definitely the right way in a tournament. The two alternatives of betting on the flop or waiting to check raise on fourth street are both quite wrong.

Betting out on the flop can be right in a side game against an aggressive player who smells weakness and will raise with almost anything. That doesn't happen nearly as much in a tournament. Thus, you should check, knowing that with that flop the raiser will almost always bet.

Waiting until fourth street to check raise gains a small bet over my suggested play when it works. The problem is that your opponent will often check the turn after you have called him on the flop, especially in a tournament. If instead your flop check raise ties him into the pot, you have gained three or even five small bets by playing the hand this way.

44. You draw a very tough table in a seven-card stud tournament. It will be many hours before it is broken up. A 2♣ brings it in. A Q♦ raises. Four others call. You have

and no nines or sevens are showing. One spade is out. What should you do?

Answer: Reraise. Normally I recommend that you stay away from close gambles. And this certainly is one. Not only are you risking more money on third street, but your raise increases the pot to a size that may well force you to gamble heavier later on. But that doesn't matter. You have a slight edge and you should push it in this spot.

Remember that the reason not to push small edges early in a tournament is because you are the best player, so it is worth giving up that edge to conserve chips against your opponents. But in this case you have little or no edge against your opponents. The players at the other tables might be a lot weaker, but you are apt to be gone before you have a chance to play against them. Had this question said that your table would be breaking up soon, I would have recommended a flat call on third street, giving up a bit of EV to ensure a decent stack size when you moved elsewhere. But with the question as stated, you can't do that.

45. Omaha high-low-split eight-or-better. You are on the button with

Three people limp in. What do you do?

Answer: Notice that I did not give any of the specifics of the situation — how many chips you or your opponents have, how they play, or how far along the tournament is. That is because it does not matter. You raise. End of story. (I have sprinkled a few questions like this throughout the quiz because I want to emphasize that strategy changes for tournaments almost always involve close plays only. This play is not close, and it would be hard to imagine a situation where you wouldn't raise.)

46. You are in the big blind with

in a no-limit hold 'em tournament. A middle position player raises your $100 blind to $400. Everyone folds. You and he both started with $5,000 in front of you. What should you do?

Answer: Against certain players you can consider flat calling. But suppose you make the more normal play of reraising. The question is, how much? The answer depends on what hands he will call various size raises with. But before we examine that, something must be pointed out. Namely, that it is disastrous to give away our hand with a small reraise. This statement is less true when we have position, but in this case it cannot be emphasized enough. The reason it is so disastrous is that he can beat us out of so many chips. Therefore, reraising say, $500, while making it obvious we have a very big pair, can't be right. It gives him too good implied odds. Knowing what we have, he will most likely lose no more when he loses, but cripple or bust us when he wins.

Might merely moving in be the right play? It sure might. Suppose, for instance, we know he will call such a move in with a pair of kings. On the other hand, if we raise $1,500, he will call with either kings or queens. Depending on post flop play, it might very well be better to move in and hope you catch him with those two kings.

The problem with moving in is that most players will fold even two kings in that spot. And it would be a shame to waste aces by just grabbing the few hundred dollars already in the pot. It would be nice to make more when he does have a decent hand. Except we don't want to give him good enough implied odds to make his call right.

If we assume that after our pre-flop reraise we always move in on the flop, it is a simple matter to calculate what that pre-flop reraise needs to be to ensure that no hand is getting good enough implied odds. Basically we are talking about him having smaller pairs. From his perspective, if you will always move in the rest of your money on the flop, his implied odds are $5,400 compared to your reraise. Do you see why?

If he calls your reraise and wins, he will beat you out of your $5,000, plus the $400 he already put in the pot. If he loses, he loses the size of your raise. That's why reraising

$500 is not enough. His implied odds are $5,400-to-$500, or almost 11-to-1, which would make calling with any pair correct. If you reraise $800, he is making a slight mistake. So slight, that given your tournament goals, you might rather he fold.

Once your reraise gets to about $1,000 you surely want him to call, knowing you'll move in on the flop. Therefore, the answer to this question is to reraise at least $1,000. But even that might not be enough if you think he is almost as likely to call a bigger reraise.

Note: Since this was originally written, players have learned to be more aggressive pre-flop while folding to reraises. Against players like these a flat call pre-flop becomes a serious contender for the best play.

47. You are playing a satellite and are down to the last two players. The blinds are $50 on the button, and $100 in front of the button. You both have $1,000 left, and he moves in on the button. You know he makes this play with any pair, but nothing else. Do you call $900 more with

Answer: Obviously no one can be figured out this perfectly. So this is really more of a math question involving the ace-king. We are also not going to adjust for the fact that you might be the better player. You don't have enough money for that skill difference to mean much, unless he is throwing way too many hands away pre-flop. The only question here is whether ace-king will win often enough against a pair to justify taking the 11-to-9 odds you are getting.

First, notice that 11-to-9 means you must win 9 out of 20 to break even. That is 45 percent. I don't want you to try to do this question absolutely perfectly. You can't bring a computer with you to the table anyway. You should come very close, however, knowing just a few facts. They are:

1. Ace-king suited is about even against two deuces.

2. Ace-king suited is about 45 percent against two queens.

3. Ace-king suited is about 34 percent against two kings.

4. Ace-king suited is about 12 percent against two aces. And,

5. Two aces and two kings come up half as often as usual — three combinations versus six — when facing an ace-king.

Let us now estimate our chances. When the opponent has a pair below kings, your chances range from 50 to 45 percent. It is only slightly inaccurate to say that your average chances against these 66 combinations of pairs are 47.5 percent. Against the two big pairs your chances are an average of 23 percent. Altogether you will win 23 percent of the six combinations of big pairs; (that is 1.38), and 47.5 percent of the 66 combinations of smaller pairs, or 31.35. Altogether you would win 32.73 out of 72 combinations.

Since 45 percent of 72 is 32.4, it looks like we barely have a call.

$$32.73 = (.475)(66) + (.23)(6)$$

$$(32.4) = (.45)(72)$$

The main reason I bothered you with this problem is to show that you cannot get too worried about running into aces or kings when you have ace-king. In this example, you are 47.5 percent when you know you are up against a pair below kings. Not knowing drops your chances down only very slightly.

48. It is the last table of a no-limit hold 'em tournament. There are five players left. The three players behind you have about $20,000 each. The player on your right has $70,000. You have $60,000. The blinds are $1,000 and $2,000. The chip leader makes it $12,000 to go under-the-gun. You have

What should you do?

Answer: Throw those two jacks away. You are not getting good enough implied odds to try to hit your set. And to try to win this hand without improving is too risky.

There are three players who will probably go broke soon. You have a good chance of coming in second, maybe first, and almost certainly, at least third. Your playing two jacks without improvement could easily result in slipping all the way to fifth. This question is a classic example of avoiding someone who can bust you in no-limit, especially when most of the other players cannot.

49. It is the middle of a limit hold 'em tournament and no one has a short stack. A tight player raises under-the-gun. The next player reraises. You are next with

What should you do?

Answer: If this is a major tournament with good players, you have an easy fold. You are getting nowhere near your odds to make a set. And if you don't make a set, you're in trouble, especially if your opponents are capable of trapping. By that I mean they check aces or kings to you when the flop comes rags. If you were all in, you would have a close decision. With money in front of you, it isn't close.

50. It's the middle of a limit hold 'em tournament. Someone raises before the flop. Someone calls. You call on the button with

The flop comes

The first player bets, the next player folds. Should you raise?

Answer: Yes. This is a routine play that is often done in the hopes of getting a free card if fourth street is a blank. The down side is that good players will often reraise which makes your strategy backfire, unless you make your hand. However, in tournaments, where most players are playing cautiously, getting reraised, even by an overpair, happens less frequently. At least that has been my experience. Thus, I would tend to make this play more in a tournament than in a side game.

Hand Quizzes

Afterthought

I suspect that many of your answers will be different from mine. This is particularly likely if you are a successful side game player with only limited (or perhaps no) tournament experience.

These "Hand Quizzes" clearly illustrate the tremendous difference between tournament poker and what you face in a normal game. You are still playing poker, but it is a different form.

So if you had some trouble with the questions, read through them again and pay special attention to where the appropriate tournament concepts come into play and where standard side game strategy "goes out the window." Don't get discouraged if many of your answers are different from mine. In time, they will be the same.

Part Five

Additional No-Limit Hold 'em Concepts (New Section)

Additional
No-Limit Hold 'em Concepts

Introduction

There are a lot of ideas that are applicable to no-limit hold 'em tournaments only. I wrote about some of them in the first edition of this book. But I didn't want to clutter up that book with too much information that didn't have applicability to all games.

Now that no-limit hold 'em has taken over the tournament scene, I've had to re-evaluate. So here I present a lot of new material about no-limit hold 'em tournaments that apply pretty much specifically to that game only. You will find most of that added material in this section.

A special section is useful because hold 'em is a unique game. In other words, it plays very differently from most other forms of poker. This is even true when you compare no-limit hold 'em to the limit form. To the uneducated eye, they look very similar — there's four rounds of betting, everyone starts with two cards, there's a three card flop, and so on. But to the experts who understand both games, they are very far apart and play almost completely differently. So in today's poker environment where no-limit hold 'em is king, this new section becomes essential for this book.

Some of what follows is slightly repetitive or possibly placed in a spot other than where it would have been if I had tried to integrate this information with the material already written. Too bad.

Don't Worry
About the "Average Stack"

As people are eliminated from the tournament, the average stack size increases accordingly. Many players put an undue emphasis on keeping up with that amount. This is a mistake, especially if it results in you playing your merely below average stacks the same way you would a short stack. In the bigger tournaments, you typically start off with 50 to 100 big blinds. You don't really have a short stack until it is below about 15 big blinds — a bit more if there is an ante. So it is easy to fall well below average and still have enough chips to play your normal game.

For instance, in the World Series of Poker, you start out with $20,000 in chips and the blinds are $50 and $100. Four hours later a third of the field is eliminated, the average stack is $30,000, and the blinds are $200 and $400. Many players who have about what they started with are feeling they have to make a move. But they are wrong. The better players understand they still have plenty of chips and do not yet have to deviate from their normal game plan.

Unlike limit games, no-limit hold 'em has a lot of short-term volatility. So even when the blinds are small, people will bust out. Which, in turn, increases the average stack size. But you don't have to be concerned with this.

One of the reasons some people begin to panic too soon in large tournaments is that there are always a few players who start off great and quickly increase their stack sizes a significant amount. So if you are below average stack size and compare your chips to one of these players, it can look like you are in trouble and need to immediately make some strategy changes. But again, this is not the case — do not deviate from your normal game plan as long as you have plenty of chips to execute it properly. Worry about the size of the blinds and the ante. Period. The rest will take care of itself.

Focus on
the Weaker Opponents

It is almost always preferable to be playing your hand against a bad player than a good player. That's obvious. But it is particularly important to lean toward confrontations with bad players, and away from confrontations with good players when you are in a tournament, and both you and your opponents have a large stack (in comparison to the blinds). This usually occurs at the beginning of the event, or even later on if you have built up your chips and there happens to be some bad players at your table who have gotten lucky enough to do the same thing.

"Bad player" can mean a few different things. Usually it means someone who plays a bit too loose, has trouble throwing away pretty good hands, and is very unlikely to make significant bluffs or semi-bluffs. It can also mean ultra-careful players who are easy to bluff-out or ultra-wild players who will often lose large amounts to you when you have a very good hand.

Obviously the correct playing strategy against these three types of players differs depending on their style. In a nutshell, you would tend to bluff the timid player, tend to save money against the non-bluffer, and seek high implied odds against the wild player. But regardless of what type of bad player they are and what type of counter strategy you should use against them, they all have one thing in common. You should play more starting hands when they are in the pot (or figure to be in the pot) than when they are not. This is especially true if both your stack and their stack is large.

Most players realize the truth of what I have just written, and already play that way. But they may not realize that these words become even more important during tournaments, especially if you are at a table that you don't expect to break for a long time.

When that is the case, it is important not only that you loosen up against these bad players, but also that you *tighten* up against the good players, especially those who also have large stacks. This is another example of the principle that it is correct to avoid slightly positive gambles for big money if a losing result costs you the opportunity to make much better gambles in the future. This principle is not only common sense, but can be verified mathematically. To get into a major confrontation with another expert when you are at such a table is just wrong, unless of course you are almost sure you have the best hand. In fact, even with the nuts, it might well be better to keep the pot small since you don't expect to get a big bet paid off.

In the next chapter, I point out that an important strategy in a no-limit hold 'em tournament is to focus on the smaller stacks when you have a much bigger one. And that is true even if the small stack is held by an expert player. With a small stack, the expert cannot use his skills, and in fact, may become so disgusted with his situation that he will play as carelessly as a bad player. But when he has a lot of chips you should be wary of him. This is always true, but it becomes that much more true when there are other players at the table who play much worse. Truer still if the table will remain in tact for many hours. (Or even if it won't, if you notice there are lots of bad players still remaining in the tournament.)

Of course, it will sometimes occur that all the live ones are gone or almost gone. If so, you must switch gears and confront those tough players head on. When you do, you may be at an advantage since they are likely to not realize that you have in fact switched gears. This edge won't last forever, so take advantage of it while you can.

Focus on the Short Stacks

Elsewhere[37] I have pointed out that players have become more and more aware of the strength of moving in their whole stack when they are short and no one else is yet in. And that you must therefore be prepared to call these move-in bets with somewhat weaker holdings than might be expected. If you do this, you can build up your stack without too much risk.

This concept can be extended to other types of hands as well. Whether your opponent is an expert or not, there are advantages to playing against him if his stack is short. Obviously this is particularly true if he plays as well or better than you. If he has a lot of chips, you should not play, as I explained in the previous chapter, close decisions against such a player if you have a lot of chips as well. But when he has a short stack, you should no longer avoid gambling with only a little bit the best of it. This can be shown mathematically. Slight edges should only be avoided if they put you in danger of missing out on bigger edges. That is not the case here.

Part of the reason for this is that in no-limit hold 'em, having a short stack also reduces some of the playing options that a highly skilled opponent might have. A simple example would be someone who is so short-stacked that he can't bluff effectively anymore. When this is the case, he is essentially transformed into the bad player who virtually never bluffs, and as already shown, that is the type of player you want to play a lot of hands against.

Of course, if the short stack is owned by a bad player, it is better yet. If for no other reason than if you double him up, you have a better chance of getting it all back later.

---

[37] See the upcoming chapter "Snapping Off All-In Moves" on page 240.

When the
Big Blind is Short or Weak

Many tournament players miss opportunities to profitably change their tactics pre-flop when the player in the big blind doesn't have very many chips or doesn't play very well. In either of these cases, you should play a few more hands than you normally would. For instance, in no-limit hold 'em, it is often correct to throw away an offsuit ace-queen, ace-jack, king-queen, or king jack. Two other marginal hands are king-ten suited and queen-ten suited. The problem with all of these hands is that they often make exactly one high pair, and one high pair is a tricky hand to play in this game. The main reason for this is that no-limit sometimes puts you in the position where you must risk many chips, and you want to avoid doing that when you only have one pair, high as it might be. Thus, when you have a big stack and are in early or middle position, you will often fold all or some of those six hands mentioned, especially in a tournament.

But folding those hands would be a mistake when the big blind is either short-stacked or doesn't play well. When he is short-stacked you won't be facing big bets on later streets because he doesn't have the chips to make those bets. When he is a bad player, especially a timid one, it doesn't matter much if he has a lot of chips because we can assume he won't bet them unless he has our one pair beaten and he is also unlikely to check raise. On the other hand, because he is a bad player, when he has something worse than us, we can often get him to pay off much larger bets with our big pair than a better player would. Notice that our positional advantage over this type of player is worth more than it would be against an opponent who plays better.

At this point you may object that we have not taken into account the fact that other players may enter the pot behind us, and that those players will often have large stacks or play well. This is a problem, but usually not that big a problem. Because if the big blind is on a short stack there will often be all-in situations with a little or no side-pot. When this occurs, even good players are not apt to try to bet you off your big pair. In the case of the big blind being a bad player, the situation is similar. This time there is no all-in pot, but there is a "protected" pot — a term I coined many years ago describing hands where you could assume a bettor was not bluffing because that bettor expected to be called by someone other than you.[38]

Another strategy change that few tournament players make, but which is actually quite profitable, occurs when you are in very late position, no one else is in, and the big blind is weak-tight. In other words he plays badly but will fold most of the time if you raise pre-flop. In these situations, if no one else is yet in, it is a horrible play to do anything but just call when you're dealt a pair of aces or kings. You could extend that to queens or jacks, ace-king suited, and other hands as well, but they are more debatable. With aces or kings a raise is terrible.

Remember we specified that the big blind was both tight and weak. So a raise costs who knows how many chips when the flop comes something like

and he folded something like

---

[38] See "The Protected Pot" starting on page 55 in *Sklansky on Poker*.

Some players might object that to just limp with aces or kings could be a recipe for disaster, as you are giving someone a free chance to flop two pairs or better. "So what," I say. That small risk is way more than made up for by the times he flops only one pair and loses a decent amount of money. Of course, it would be even more correct to make this play when the big blind stack is not large enough to hurt you, but either way it should be done. If he does have a big stack and risks much of it, you, as a good player, should usually recognize the times to get away from your over pair. (Obviously in the case of you having two kings, a mere ace on the flop messes up your plans, but again it is a risk worth taking.)

When the
Antes are All You Need

There are many tournaments, especially big ones, where it is not unusual to find a table with players so tight that mere ante stealing can show a profit, or at least keep you close to even. When you find yourself at such a table it is imperative that you recognize the situation, take advantage of it, and in many cases adjust your post-flop play as well.

Typically, you will find tables like this at about the time the ante is first introduced. In other words, say the previous round was a $100 and $200 blind, and this round the blinds remain the same, but there is now a $25 ante. So in a nine-handed game there will be $525 in the pot to start. Notice that a $600 opening raise will show an immediate profit if it succeeds 53 percent of the time.

$$0 = (X)(\$525) - (1 - X)(\$600)$$
$$= \$525X - \$600 + \$600X \Rightarrow$$

$$\$1,125X = \$600 \Rightarrow$$

$$X = \frac{\$600}{\$1,125} = .533$$

That same raise would require a 67 percent chance of success without the ante to show an immediate profit.

$$0 = (X)(\$300) - (1 - X)(\$600)$$
$$= \$300X - \$600 + \$600X \Rightarrow$$

$$\$900X = \$600 \Rightarrow$$

$$X = \frac{\$600}{\$900} = .6667$$

Of course, both those numbers are conservative since they assume that you will always lose and always give up if the ante steal fails. If instead you use the strategy of giving up unless you flop a good hand, you need not succeed as often with your steals to make it a profitable play.

Let's look at a simplistic example. Simplistic because I am not taking into account your position, the strength of your hand, and a few other things. But it still captures the essence of what I am talking about. We will continue to use this $100-$200 blind and $25 ante example.

Suppose you are at a table that respects your raises to the point where you realize that the table as a whole will fold about half the time if you bring it in pre-flop for $600. That's simply too much folding on their part. And you must take advantage of it.

However, you shouldn't take advantage too much. If you do, your opponents will realize it and adjust accordingly. So say you decide to add two extra hands per round to your raising "menu." In other words, you play most of your hands normally, but you choose two extra mediocre hands to throw in such a raise. Each time you raise you pick up $525 when they fold. The other half the time you have the worst of it. But it's certainly not a $600 loss. If you are a good player you should easily be able to keep your average loss, when called, down to $300. The bottom line is that these two extra pre-flop raising hands earn you $112.50 each in EV.

$$\$112.50 = \left(\frac{1}{2}\right)(\$525) - \left(\frac{1}{2}\right)(\$300)$$

That's $225 above and beyond what your normal play would earn.

In fact, this extra $225 per round is so significant it means that if you can count on it for a long period of time you should seriously consider playing much more carefully when you are playing other hands. This would be obvious if the edge was even greater. If your two extra hands had a 90 percent chance of stealing, you could fold every other hand and still guarantee winning the tournament. So there would be no reason not to. Of course, the real edge is nowhere near this big, but it doesn't have to be to make your overall post-flop strategy tighter when the antes are just asking to be stolen.

Implication of the Modern Tournament Prize Structure

Let's now take a quick look at one aspect of the prize structures nowadays and how it affects you. In an effort to pay as many people as possible, while not reducing the top prizes too much, tournament officials are paying approximately twice the buy-in to about ten percent of the field, but very little above that until you reach the top one per cent or so.

Thus in a 1,000 player $1,500 buy-in no-limit hold 'em tournament, 100th place could pay about $3,000, but barely increases until you get to the final table. This has the effect of keeping more people in money so they can buy into additional tournaments, and it makes for a larger number of players leaving the tournament with a positive feeling. And tournament organizers can advertise big payouts for their winners and help keep their events full.

In this example, first prize would be over a quarter of a million. But that drops down quickly. The average prize for those who make the final table is at best $60,000. No more than twenty times the 100th prize.

The end result of these facts is that when you are very near the bubble you are hurting yourself pretty badly, EV wise, if you gamble all your chips with a slight edge. And this becomes truer and truer as your stack becomes smaller and smaller (unless your stack is so tiny that you have little chance of reaching the money without winning a pot).

To make these ideas more precise, let's look at a simplified scenario that makes the calculations easy. But in spite of its simplicity, I still think it does a pretty good job of capturing the essence of the situation. Although it does perhaps slightly exaggerate things.

Rather than giving away 100 prizes, let's give away ten. Second through tenth place gets $100. First gets $2,000. Eleven players are left. One of them is desperately short and will almost certainly be gone in a few hands.

At this point the chip leader moves all in. Ignore the antes. Assume you are getting even money. Everyone else has folded. From a pure math standpoint, what chance of winning do you need to make a call correct?

Like I said, the answer depends on how many chips you have. Say you have 30 percent of the chips at this point. That means that your EV before the hand started was 30 percent of $2,000 representing those times you expect to win the tournament plus 70 percent of $100 representing those times you finish second through tenth, or $670.

$$\$670 = (.30)(\$2,000) + (.70)(\$100)$$

If you call and lose, you go broke and lose that $670.

If instead you call and win, your EV moves up to 60 percent of $2,000 plus 40 percent of $100. That's $1,240.

$$\$1,240 = (.60)(\$2,000) + (.40)(\$100)$$

which is an increase of $570.

$$\$570 = \$1,240 - \$670$$

So you are laying $670 to win $570. Thus you need to be about 54 percent to call.

But what about if you have only 5 percent of the chips? Right now your equity is 5 percent of $2,000 plus 95 percent of $100 or $195.

$$\$195 = (.05)(\$2,000) + (.95)(\$100)$$

Double up and it moves to 10 percent of $2,000 plus 90 percent of $100. That's $290.

$$\$290 = (.10)(\$2,000) + (.90)(\$100)$$

which is an increase of $95.

$$\$95 = \$290 - \$195$$

Calling means risking your $195 equity to win $95 more in EV.

So in this case you really need to be approximately a 2-to-1 favorite to consider calling. Even with average chips (10 percent), doubling your chips only increases your equity by about 60 percent (from $290 to $460).

In actual tournament conditions, the effects illustrated here are not quite this extreme. You are getting pot odds. No player is certain to go broke if you opt to not play. First prize is more than twenty times last prize. On the other hand, that last prize may be very significant to you. Especially if you got in the tournament via satellite or your bankroll is a little smaller than you would like it to be.

The bottom line is that these prize structures really force you to make a decision. Do you maximize your EV by making sure you don't get broke near the bubble? Or do you maximize your chance of making the big score? Only you can answer that. But if you do choose the second option, and find yourself at a table with those who choose the first, I would hope it's not necessary for me to tell you what you should be doing, i.e. stealing from them..

By the way, in the tournament world, you'll often hear players state that since the big money is in the first three places, you shouldn't adjust your strategy until you get close to the big money. While it is true that the chips change value more the closer you get to first place, this concept can also impact correct strategy well before you reach the final table.

The Stop 'n Go Play

This fairly well known play mainly occurs when you're in the big blind. It may also occur when you raise pre-flop and get reraised. If your chip stack is such that moving in pre-flop will virtually always get called, you should consider another option. What you should sometimes do is simply call before the flop and then move in on the flop. Typically, this play is better those times your hand is not that strong.

Of course, your hand does need to be strong enough to make your call of his raise correct. In fact, for this stop and go play to be right, it is usually necessary that moving in pre-flop on your part would have had a positive EV. It's just that waiting for the flop to come down before you bet might have an even greater EV. Here's a fairly simple example. Suppose the blinds are $100 and $200, the ante is $25, and the table is eight-handed. You are in the big blind with

and have $1,000 behind you. The button makes it $600 to go and you know he will do this with any two cards.

The small blind folds. At this moment you are getting $1,100-to-$400 odds. If you move in for your $1,000 and he calls you, you are getting $1,700-to-$1,000 odds. Obviously moving in is a profitable play. You will win this pot about half the time if he calls you. And of course he will call because on your last raise he is getting $2,100-to-$600 odds. So to many players this situation is a slam dunk reraise, a slam dunk call, and a coin flip for a

$2,700 pot. And when the smoke clears the pair of deuces will average having $1,350 in their stack. The play seems simple and right. But it isn't.

Against virtually all opponents, the better play is to just call the $400 raise and then bet $600 on the flop, except possibly if a deuce comes. When you do this, you are offering your opponent odds of $2,100-to-600, or 3½-to-1. And unless he has a deuce in his hand, those are odds he should take. But he often won't. If the flop is

he will not be calling with an

as well as much better hands than that. In fact, a good proportion of the flops that do not hit him will cause him to fold when you bet $600, even though, unbeknownst to him, he has six wins and is only about a 3-to-1 underdog.

I am not going to bore you with the math, but hopefully you see that if your strategy will have you either putting in all your money pre-flop or on the flop, and if your opponent will sometimes incorrectly fold when you wait for the flop to come down, your EV will improve by waiting.

Keep in mind that for the stop and go play to be the preferred play, you need to have some chance that your opponent will incorrectly fold on the flop. Furthermore, it is important that he will rarely correctly fold. That's why, in this example, if you have a pair of eights rather than the deuces, it is almost definitely better to move in pre-flop. If he has a card lower than an eight in his hand and he flops nothing, you have cost yourself EV if you opt not to move in before the flop, and then your flop bet makes him fold.

Here's one more example. Again the blinds are $100 and $200. The ante is $25. The table is eight handed. You are in the big blind with $1,000 behind, and the button makes it $600 to go probably with any two cards. And your hand is Q♦7♠. It's well known that a queen-seven against two random cards wins approximately 50 percent of the time, so you should certainly play. But by executing the stop and go play, your opponent may throw away some king-high hands plus some hands which, while not as good as your queen-high, would be getting the right price to call your flop bet.

Obviously this subject could be analyzed in very great detail. However, knowing those details would only add a little bit to what a general understanding of the play does for you already.

Some Unusual
Plays with Aces and Kings

You're only dealt aces or kings about 1 percent of the time. Most players do not get the most out of them because they have too great a fear of letting somebody else draw out. But that's silly. With two aces, any individual opponent only has about a 15 percent chance of beating you even if there is no bet the whole way through. So it is often correct to take this chance. Obviously with two kings, your risk is greater. On the other hand, when your kings are beaten, it is usually because an ace comes on the board so you usually lose a lot less than when your aces are beaten.

Here are three examples of unusual plays that should often be made pre-flop with these hands:

1. **Flat call a reraise.** If you raise before the flop with two aces (or possibly two kings) and an opponent reraises, consider flat calling, especially if it is heads up. If you reraise here, you have pretty much given your hand away and your opponent will often fold immediately. When he doesn't, your pre-flop reraise will frequently cost you money on later streets. For instance, if he has

and the flop is destined to be

you almost certainly will win more had you not raised a second time pre-flop. This would be even more true if he reraised with a hand like

Exactly when and when not to make this play is a bit tricky and depends on specific circumstances. One disadvantage of flat-calling is, of course, that you give him a free shot to beat you. Another one is that sometimes the flop will come down in such a way that you wish you had gotten your money in earlier; the obvious example being where he has two kings and the flop comes with an ace. Still, all in all, I believe that in a heads up situation, the right pre-flop play is usually to call, especially with aces.

In fact, this play can even be extended to those cases where you hadn't raised originally. For instance, when you are in the big blind, and your lone opponent has raised pre-flop or when you limp in and your lone opponent raises. Just remember to consider all these factors.

2. **Two kings early in a tournament against a typical raise.** This play involves a specific situation and specific hand. But

I see it misplayed all the time. It is the beginning of the tournament, players are trying to play tight and well, and the stacks are large and the blinds are small. Someone in early position opens for a typical raise, three to five times the size of the big blind. You are in early position behind him and have a pair of kings. At most tables, reraising is wrong.

Think about it. If you reraise you will usually win the pot right there, and that's an irrelevant pot. It's not going to help you win this tournament. If you just call, there is a chance for much greater gains. You have position on the raiser, and if he is allowed to stay in, he will often lose a decent amount with pairs under kings. Or he might try to bluff on the flop (or on the turn if you both check the flop).

An additional good thing that can happen if you make this play is that a pretty good hand behind you which would have folded had you raised, might now raise themselves. If the original raiser just calls, now you can make a big reraise.

However, another reason to make this play of just calling with your kings is that it is easily possible the original raiser has two aces. If this is a tight player, he might only raise with aces down through nines, or ace-king. That means there is more than a 10 percent chance he actually does have aces. If you raise here and he just calls as I suggested earlier, you will lose a lot more than if you had called. The same is true if he reraises a small amount. (If he reraises a larger amount, you will be able to get away from the kings, but simultaneously, you miss the chance of perhaps taking all his chips if you flop or turn a set.)

There are of course arguments in favor of making this reraise pre-flop even in this early stage of the tournament. But in most cases, those arguments are not as strong as the arguments in favor of just calling.

3. **At an aggressive table.** I have spoken about this before, but don't think it can be over-emphasized. When you are at a

table that is aggressive, even moderately so, it may well be worth it to limp in with aces and kings, even in fairly late position, and even when multiple players have already limped in in front of you. All that is necessary is that stacks be large relative to the blinds and antes and some of the players behind you be greedy.

When you make this play and someone behind you, often a greedy big blind, who would have folded decides to raise himself, the swing in equity between the two plays is enormous. He raises, and perhaps gets a call or two, and now you reraise. This is so much better than if you yourself raise and simply take the pot, as you probably will. (In fact, some players when in the big blind can't resist putting in a large raise regardless of their hand.)

Even if no one does raise, it is not necessarily true that you cost yourself money. Since a raise usually takes the pot immediately, your mere call opens up opportunities to win more post-flop. Obviously, this money will come mainly those times when you flop sets. But if you have a nice skill edge over your opponents, it will often come when you flop a mere overpair as well.

Many so-called experts will recommend against this play because they worry that an overpair can cost you a lot of money when many players see the flop. But I'm making the assumption that you are a good player and can thus limit your losses when you have a second-best hand. If you can, the upsides of making this deep limping play with aces or kings should more than make up for the downsides.

Moving-In
Against the Blind[39]

I mentioned earlier that one talent tournament pros have that side game pros might not is the understanding of all-in situations. The following mathematical problem is a good example of the thinking tournament players should have a firm grasp of.

You are on the button holding

All have folded to you. For simplicity's sake we will say that there is only one blind of $100. The guy in the blind has more money than you.

Although flat calling could conceivably be the best play, especially if your stack is large, this problem will analyze only the two options of folding or moving in.

What we will do is postulate three different opponents. Player A will call with ace-king, ace-queen, or any pair. Player B will call with ace-king, ace-queen, or sevens or better. Player C will call with ace-king, ace-queen, or tens or better. Against each of these opponents it would obviously be more profitable to move in than fold unless your stack was very big. But there is a stack size

---

[39] This chapter was originally an article in the *Two Plus Two Internet Magazine* at www.twoplustwo.com. It covers material that was also discussed earlier. But the subject is important so a little repetition can't hurt.

in each case where moving in becomes negative EV. Let's do the calculations.

First, let's take the case of the opponent who needs a pair of sevens or ace-king or ace-queen to call. That's 80 combinations (six each of the eight possible pairs and sixteen each of the two possible non-pairs). You will then be called 80 out of 1,225 times.

$$80 = (8)(6) + (2)(16)$$

$$1,225 = \frac{(50)(49)}{2}$$

When you are called you will win about 23 of the 80 times. See why? Thus if you move in \$X 1,225 times you will win \$100 1,145 times, win \$X 23 times, and lose \$X 57 times. The point at which the move in no longer shows a profit is when

$$\$0 = (1,145)(\$100) + (23)(\$X) - (57)(\$X) \Rightarrow$$

$$(34)(\$X) = \$114,500 \Rightarrow$$

$$X = \$3,367.65$$

That's over 33 big blinds.

Now let's calculate against the opponent who needs ace-king, ace-queen, or tens or better to call. But before doing this, I want you to stop and think whether the answer should be more or less than 33 blinds.

This time your opponent will call with only 62 out of 1,225 hands and you will win 20 of those 62. Moving in \$X, your result after 1,225 hands will be

$$\$0 = (1{,}163)(\$100) + (20)(\$X) - (42)(\$X) \Rightarrow$$

$$(22)(\$X) = \$116{,}300 \Rightarrow$$

$$X = \$5{,}286.36$$

That's almost 53 big blinds.

Hopefully, you see that the reason this result is greater than the first question's answer is because the opponent is throwing away hands (nines, eights, and sevens) that you are very happy to have him fold.

Now use similar logic to deduce for yourself whether the amount you can profitably move in with is higher or lower than 53 big blinds if your opponent will call your move in (when you hold two sixes) with *any* pair as well as ace-king or ace-queen.

There are now 105 combinations of hands that he will call with — includes one combination of six-six. You will win about 43½ of them (counting one tie as a half of a win). The equation is thus:

$$\$0 = (1{,}120)(\$100) + (43.5)(\$X) - (61.5)(\$X) \Rightarrow$$

$$(18)(\$X) = \$112{,}000 \Rightarrow$$

$$X = \$6{,}222.22$$

That's about 62 big blinds.

Again, I'm hoping that you realize that you can be even more liberal in your raises in this situation than in the previous one because the player, while no longer making the error of folding sevens, eights, and nines, will also now make the costly play of calling with fives down through deuces which result overall in a bigger "mistake" ("Fundamental Theory of Poker" wise[40]) than calling with only tens or higher.

Please understand that to make the calculation simple I gave you a way better than average hand, namely a pair of sixes. With that hand you need a lot of chips before moving in is a worse play than folding would be. Though a call or small raise might be better still.

But the principle is the same with a hand like

or

when you have a moderate stack and moving in or folding are the only legitimate alternatives. In these cases, your first thought should be how much can you move in profitably if your opponent will call you with those hands that he should, if he saw your hand, and fold correctly with the rest of the hands he's dealt (again assuming that he saw your hand). Armed with this information, you can revise the figure upward depending on how many (and which) of the hands that he should call with he will in fact

---

[40] See *The Theory of Poker* by David Sklansky for more discussion.

probably fold, as well as how many hands he should fold that he would "incorrectly" call with.

Note: This subject will be further expanded upon in the upcoming chapter "Two Wonderful Charts" on page 252.

Snapping Off All-In Moves

Nowadays many tournament players are aware of the value of first-in, all-in, pre-flop bets with a moderately short stack. They know that even if their hand is fairly weak, it is profitable to move in stacks up to ten times the amount of money in the pot because of their two ways of winning — instantly most of the time, or when they are called. When they make this play, they know that if they in fact do get called, their hand is probably an underdog. But if they can win a third of those times, and get away with the ante-blind steal perhaps 80 percent of the time, it's still a winning play.

Because of the widespread knowledge of this idea, it is more and more common to see shorter stacks moving in with rather weak hands when no one else is yet in. In fact, many players will reserve this move for their mediocre starting hands and raise a smaller amount with their best ones. The net result is that it doesn't take that good a hand to be a favorite over the average hand players in this situation will push with. This means you should seriously consider calling such a bet with less than a super premium hand. This includes hands like ace-jack, king-queen, a pair of sevens, or possibly even slightly worse.

If you have a borderline decision, other factors to consider are your own stack size, how many players are yet to act behind you, the size of his raise, and the position he was in when he made the play. The most important would be the second factor, the number of players still to act after you.

If there are many players yet to act, you'll need to fold quite a few more hands. You should also be slightly more apt to fold if the all-in player is in early position, if his bet is fairly large, or if you yourself have a fairly short stack. The best time to make this call is when your stack is large, your short-stacked opponent is on the button or in the small blind, and you are on the big blind.

Here's a very simple example. The blinds are $200 and $400, any you are in the big blind with K♥Q♦. Your lone opponent has moved all-in from late position for $1,800. You should call assuming you have a big stack. On the other hand, if your opponent made this same all-in raise from early position and you were on his immediate left, your play would be to fold.

The Gap Concept
Doesn't Always Apply

When I first wrote this book, I had no idea that no-limit hold 'em would catch fire as a tournament game. Because of that, I neglected to mention that there is a significant exception to the Gap Concept discussed elsewhere in this book. To refresh your memory, it was pointed out that the well-known gap between opening requirements and calling requirements increases in a tournament. The reason is that players are frequently playing tighter and trying to survive.

This idea is just as true at certain stages of no-limit hold 'em tournaments as it is in any other kind of tournament. In fact, it is often even more true. For instance, if stacks are small and an ante is added, first-in move-ins should frequently be made with rather weak hands and calls of those move-ins should only be made with very good hands. This is pure math and is not open for debate. When you get to the final table, and most players have a relatively short stack, this concept is stronger still. "First-in equity" is ridiculously strong. I explain this idea in more detail in the upcoming chapter on "Sit 'n Go Tournaments" starting on page 265. These tournaments essentially duplicate last table situations.

But there are times when it is wrong to abide by the Gap Concept. Those times occur when the players in the pot have a lot of chips compared to the blinds. This is especially true if you are a no-limit hold 'em expert. When such is the case you should often call a moderate raise pre-flop with hands that are obviously worse than what you think the raiser has. Or, for that matter, with hands that are worse than what you yourself would have raised with in his position. Perhaps king-nine suited, eight-six suited, or even jack-ten offsuit. These are all hands that you would normally throw away in early position, yet against mediocre predictable players or perhaps even good players you might consider calling in late position when you are behind them.

The reason for this is of course the dramatic advantage which accrues to you when you have position on your opponent, especially if you are an expert at playing big stacks. Most world class players are well aware of this exception to the Gap Concept and use it to their advantage. Now you will be too.

When Chips
Don't Lose Value

I have emphasized many times in this book that tournament strategy usually requires you to avoid close gambles for large portions of your chips. The slightly positive EV of such a gamble doesn't make up for the fact that you are risking losing chips that could have been risked in more advantageous situations. Put into more mathematical terminology, chips lose value as they increase.

But there are sometimes exceptions. The obvious ones are when you are not at a good table or you are not that great a player. If you don't think you have a nice overall edge on your opponents, then there is no reason to pass up any edge that does come your way, at least not in the beginning or middle stages of the tournament. (If you are lucky enough to make the money, there are situations discussed elsewhere where even a mediocre player should avoid a close gamble.)

What is less obvious is that even great players are sometimes in a position where their chips do not lose value. In other words, where a doubling of their chips more than doubles their overall equity. And of course, when they are in that situation they should not avoid and even seek out "coin flip" situations. I touched upon this in another section, but I'd like to get a little more explicit here. When a great player has a very small stack, he no longer has plus EV with those chips.

I don't want to get too technical, but I do want you to understand the basics behind that last sentence. In "Should You Wait" which starts on page 97 in my book, *Sklansky on Poker,* I demonstrate that one should refrain from making a slightly good bet if a better bet for the same stakes is on the horizon, and you will be broke if you make and lose the first bet. It's a simple algebra problem which results in a formula describing exactly how good the first bet must be compared to the second bet in order to make it right to make that first bet. But what's interesting about this formula is that when you use it in situations where the upcoming bet is a bad bet, yet is one that you must make, the formula will tell you to make the first bet even if it has a somewhat negative EV. The idea is that it is better to make a poor bet now, than a terrible bet later.

In no-limit hold 'em tournaments you are often in this second situation. The blinds are coming up. You're continually putting antes in the pot. And if your stack is short you will usually have to make a stand, particularly when the big blind reaches you, with a hand you don't want to play. Put another way, when you do have the big blind your EV will be substantially negative. And if you lose that hand you will be unable to regain that EV from subsequent hands when others are in the blind because you are broke and you can't buy in again. This explanation is not totally rigorous, but I think you get the idea. And the bottom line is that no matter how well you play, if your stack falls below a certain point, your equity for that tournament falls below the proportion of chips you have.

Here's an example. Suppose with 1 percent of all the chips you estimate your equity at 1.5 percent of the prize money. And with 5 percent of the chips you estimate your equity at 7 percent of the prize money. Notice that quintupling your chips has not quintupled your equity. So extra chips have lost value. But now let's say that your stack is only .2 percent of all the chips. For the reasons given above, your desperate situation may mean that your equity is only .18 percent of the total prize money. If that is the case, we see that quintupling those chips would multiply your equity by about 8. Your chips would gain value if they increased. And when you are in that situation it is obviously correct to bet as much as you can with little or no edge.

Exactly how small your stack has to be before you fall into this strange situation where chips don't lose value is not an easy question. It depends on your skill, whether there is an ante, and how soon and how high the next level will be. I would estimate the point is somewhere between 15 and 30 times the big blind. But it could be higher.

Here's an obvious example. You're dealt

under-the-gun and are very low on chips of which the big blind will consume a fair proportion of if you throw this hand away. So even though you know that under normal circumstances you should fold because your expectation is negative, it turns out that your overall expectation is less negative to play this hand (usually by moving all-in) than to fold and then post your big blind.

Why No-Limit Hold 'em Cash Game Experts Sometimes Do Poorly at No-Limit Hold 'em Tournaments

In "Tournament Experts Versus Live Game Experts" starting on page 109 in "Part Three: Other Topics" I addressed this issue. But it turns out that the disparity between cash game skills and tournament skills, which exists for all games, reaches its peak in the specific game of no-limit hold 'em. That is being an excellent no-limit hold 'em cash game player does not guarantee success in no-limit hold 'em tournaments. So I want to readdress this issue here with the emphasis on specifically no-limit hold 'em.

Many great no-limit hold 'em players struggle with tournaments for the following reasons:

1. **They are not used to playing with antes.** The majority of no-limit hold 'em tournaments force players to put in an ante as well as blinds after the first few rounds. Cash games rarely have an ante. The change in proper strategy when an ante is added is sometimes significant since the immediate odds the pot is offering you are greater.

2. **Cash game players rarely have to deal with short stacks or pre-flop move-ins.** In cash games, almost all players have a significant number of chips compared to the blinds. This means that post-flop play is where the experts figure to earn most of their money. In tournaments however, players are frequently confronted with opponents who are on a short stack or situations where they themselves have a short stack. The right strategy in these situations is basically technical and mathematical. It is not based as much on feel, intuition, or general poker skill. Those cash game players who have not

studied the technicalities involved will be at a disadvantage against players who have, even players with lesser overall "poker" skill.

3. **Tournaments are often composed of bad players.** Many cash game players are not used to playing against the various types of weak players that are encountered in a tournament. Many of these types of weak players shy away from high-stakes side games. I'm not suggesting that a cash game pro would actually be an underdog against these players; his problem is that he won't be as much of a favorite as tournament specialists who are experienced in extracting the maximum from these weaker players. Thus when the smoke clears, the tournament specialist figures to have amassed a greater stack than the cash game specialist. This is an advantage that more than makes up for the fact that the cash pro plays a bit better than the tournament pro. This is especially true because it is rare that a player, except at the beginning of a tournament, will ever have a deep enough stack and be against deep enough stacks where cash game skills shine.

4. **Weak players play differently in tournaments than they do in cash games.** Even when cash game players have experience playing weaker players, that experience doesn't serve them well when it comes to tournaments. That's because weaker players often play quite a bit differently when they are in a tournament than when they are in a cash game. They still play badly, but maybe not in the way that a cash game specialist would expect.

5. **Cash game specialists may not understand tournament theory.** I'm speaking of the general principle of avoiding close gambles for all your chips when your stack is large and your edge is small. I'm also speaking of the exception to that

rule, when your stack has fallen below a certain point. Both these concepts are examined in detail in various places in this book. But some cash game players are moronic enough not to have read it.

6. **Cash game specialists know nothing of prize money theory.** The differences in proper strategy between cash games and tournaments increases further when a player is in the money or near the money. Sometimes these differences are extreme. It can even be correct to throw away two aces before the flop. Again, this has been discussed in detail elsewhere, but illiterate cash game experts are apt to make significant mistakes in these situations.

How Amateurs
Should Play the
Deep-Stacked Early Rounds

I have emphasized in many places in this book the idea that the best players should be cautious early on, while the weaker players should not. The idea being that great players' edges accumulate as time goes by, and that highly advantageous situations are apt to arise if you wait long enough. For both these reasons, it is simply wrong for great players to risk a significant portion of their stack in only slightly positive EV situations.

For weaker players however, the opposite is normally true. Their edges won't accumulate, and they are less likely to recognize better opportunities in the future. Thus, these players should be willing to risk lots of chips with any slight edge, especially if that involves putting pressure on those great players who are trying to avoid such confrontations.

But there is sort of an exception to all of this. It occurs at the very beginning of large tournaments. When stacks are very deep, great players should in fact loosen up, and play quite liberally. If stacks are 50 or more times the big blind, the best players tend to have the greatest edge. This should be no surprise, because with stacks this deep there is opportunity to use poker skill on all betting rounds. In fact, when the stacks are this deep, the correct strategy is very similar to correct cash game strategy. And it is in these very early rounds where you often see the best players, especially those with good strong cash game skills, doubling or even tripling up.

These experts are not really violating tournament principles when they splash around like this because those principles admonish against great players risking *large* amounts of chips with small edges. At the beginning of a tournament (or even later on if the player happens to have attained many more chips), this splashing around only involves a small percentage of their stack.

(This splashing around with large stacks relative to the blinds even has a name among the tournament regulars. It is referred to as "small ball," and is nothing more than playing expert deep stack no-limit hold 'em.)

But what of the less than great player? The normal rules also reverse for him. Since he cannot outplay his opponents for a large amount of chips in comparison to his stack, he shouldn't gamble at all. His problem is that if he gets involved with marginal hands, he still has lots of chips at risk on the later rounds. And in the later rounds there are far fewer coin flip type situations which means the expert will often find ways to have a big edge against him in those rounds.

If you are truly an amateur or beginner, taking my advice to play very tightly when your stack is deep is not going to help you much. But if instead you are a mediocre cash player but have a good understanding of tournament theory, including the mathematics of playing short stacks, taking this advice is critical. Remember those cash game players we talked about in the previous chapter? As stacks diminish in comparison to the increasing blinds, and as antes are added, your disadvantage against these players shrinks or even disappears all together.

The bottom line is that if you are a decent tournament player and understand the theories presented in this book, but you are not that good a cash game player, you should consider playing ultra-tight if you are at a tough table those first few rounds. I could almost go as far as to say you shouldn't show up at all. Obviously that advice is dubious since you miss the opportunity to be dealt two aces or to get in cheaply with a pair or a suited ace, and then flop a set or a flush. But if you did show up and restricted your play to only those situations, I wouldn't have a problem with it. Don't try to box early on with the experts. Back-peddle until round three or so, and then start going for knock-out punches.

Two Wonderful Charts

As a poker author my main goal is to turn novices into excellent players. Players who can beat most games for serious money. But it is unrealistic for me to expect that I can turn a novice into a truly great world-class player. In other words, I can't seriously expect that my books will often teach you things that the great players don't already know.

But there are exceptions, and this chapter contains two of them. Two charts that give information that is not only very useful in no-limit tournaments, but is also information that even the greatest players usually do not have (unless, of course, they have read my books).

I say "my books" rather than "this book" because the charts were originally printed in *No-Limit Hold 'em: Theory and Practice* which I wrote with Ed Miller, a book that was geared more toward cash games than tournaments. Presumably you have that book, or if you don't you will soon be getting it. However, for convenience, Two Plus Two Publishing LLC has given permission to reprint the charts here.

Both charts involve pre-flop move-ins. As I've stated elsewhere, that type of bet is a very powerful tool. This is even more true in tournaments than in side-games because there is often an ante, and stacks are frequently smaller compared to blinds than they are in a cash game. The specific move that will be analyzed is the pre-flop move-in when no one else is in yet. If the move-in occurs behind a limp or a raise, these charts can still be used as a guideline in the hands of expert players. But that is not their main function.

As stated often in this text, moving in moderate-size stacks to steal the blinds, and sometimes the antes, is almost never a real bad play. This is doubly true when you are facing players who figure to be better than you on the later rounds. If you have a moderate stack, perhaps as much as ten times what is in the pot already, a move in open is clearly wrong with trash and perhaps with a pair of aces. Anything else is reasonably okay. Especially against tighter players who will respect that raise.

When I first broached this subject in the original edition of this book, the idea was fairly unknown, and somewhat revolutionary. Similar to the revolutionary idea that Edward Thorpe wrote about in *Beat The Dealer* when he showed that you should often double-down in blackjack with hands like ace-four. But now everyone knows about this move all-in play. In fact, a whole book was written about it —*Kill Phil* by Blair Rodman and Lee Nelson.

What's important to understand is that pre-flop move-ins is a subject that is almost purely mathematical. There is a bit of non-mathematical poker skill involved, regarding putting your opponent on a range of hands, but after you do that, it's all math. If you don't know what the math tells you, you are at a big disadvantage compared to those who do. And the following two charts go a long way to show you exactly what you need to know.

The Calling Chart

When someone moves in before the flop and it is up to you to call, the basic idea is that you should make that call if your pot odds are favorable compared to your chances of winning. Of course, you might consider folding slightly favorable situations if the number of chips is significant, and you feel like you're better than most of the players at the table. Another reason to fold is when the math says it's close and if there are players yet to act behind you. These two factors are not taken into account in the following chart, but it is a simple matter to make this small adjustment when necessary.

The chart assumes you are in the big blind, are raised by one person, and everybody else is out. It also assumes that you or he is all-in. The chart enumerates three possibilities regarding the possible pot odds you are getting, 2-to-1, 3-to-2, or 6-to-5. There is no reason to deal with odds above 2-to-1 since they rarely occur, and when they do, you should usually call with anything. Less than 6-to-5 is likewise irrelevant since it again is a rare situation and the odds can never fall below even money. If the odds you're getting are something between 6-to5 and 3-to-2, or between 3-to-2 and 2-to-1, you need to do a little bit of interpolation, but that should be simple enough.

If you knew exactly what your opponent had it would be easy to decide whether your pot odds justify a call. The problem is you don't. Even the most predictable player can have a few different hands when he makes this move-in. And that complicates things a lot; partly because you cannot simply average out your chances against his various hands. The reason you can't average them out is that certain hands are dealt more often than others. This means you must take a *weighted* average. Furthermore, you must adjust his card combination possibilities based on the cards you're holding in your hand. So there is no way you can be expected to make an accurate estimation in the heat of battle at the table, even if you are quite sure of your opponent's hand ranges and you know all your poker math. Thus you first need to become familiar with the following table.

What this chart tells you specifically are the hands that will show an EV profit calling an all-in raise getting those three different types of pot odds against five different types of raisers: very tight, tight, average, loose, and any two.

Here's is how we define those five types of raisers:

Table I: The Hand Range Categories

Very tight (3%)	AA-JJ and AK
Tight (5%)	AA-99 and AK-AQ
Average (10%)	AA-77, AK-AT, and KQ
Loose (25%)	AA-22, AK-A5, Any two cards T or higher (e.g., QT), and K9s-T9s
Very loose (50%)	AA-22, AK-A2, Any two cards 7 or higher (e.g., T7), K6-K4, and K3s-K2s
Any two (100%)	Everything

Now here's the Calling Chart.

Table II: The Hand Ranges for Calling

	6-to-5	3-to-2	2-to-1
Very Tight (3%)	AA-QQ	AA-QQ, AKs	AA-TT, AK
Tight (5%)	AA-JJ, AK	AA-TT, AK	AA-22, AK-AQ, AJs, KJs-KTs (not KQs), QJs-JTs
Average (10%)	AA-99, AK-AQ, AJs	AA-55, AK-AJ, ATs	AA-22, AK-AT, A9s-A2s, KQ, KJs-K9s, QJs-Q9s, JTs-54s, J9s-97s, J8s
Loose (25%)	AA-44, AK-A8, A7s, KQ, KJs-KTs	AA-22, AK-A2, KQ-KT, K9s-K6s, QJ, QTs-Q9s, JTs	AA-22, AK-A2, KQ-K2, QJ-Q6, Q5s-Q2s, JT-J8, J7s-J2s, T9-T8, T7s-T3s, 98-97, 96s-93s, 87-86, 85s-84s, 76, 75s-73s, 65, 64s-63s, 54s-52s, 43s-42s

Very loose (50%)	AA-22, AK-A2, KQ-K7, K6s-K5s, QJ-QT, Q9s-Q8s, JT, J9s	AA-22, AK-A2, KQ-K2, QJ-Q7, Q6s-Q2s, JT-J8, J7s-J6s, T9, T8s-T7s, 98s	AA-22, AK-A2, KQ-K2, QJ-Q2, JT-J2, T9-T3, 98-95, 87-85, 76-75, 65-64, 54-53, Any two suited except 72s
Any two (100%)	AA-22, AK-A2, KQ-K2, QJ-Q2, JT-J4, J3s-J2s, T9-T7, T6s-T3s, 98-97, 96s-95s, 87s-86s	AA-22, AK-A2, KQ-K2, QJ-Q2, JT-J2, T9-T2, 98-93, 92s, 87-85, 84s-82s, 76-75, 74s-73s, 65s-64s, 54s	Everything except 42o-32o

If you think the raiser is in-between categories, you would again interpolate slightly from what you see in the chart. If you think the raiser would *not* move all-in with specifically two aces or perhaps kings, you can loosen up your calling requirements, but perhaps surprisingly, only by a slight amount.

Let's try one example to make sure you get the idea. Suppose the blinds are $100-$200. The ante is $25. And the game is eight handed. You are the big blind and have $1,000 more left. A middle position player brings it in for $900. Everyone else folds. You look down and see

You assess this player as an "average"raiser. In other words he has a pair of aces down through sevens, ace-king down through ace-ten, or king-queen.

It's $700 to you, so he's not putting you all-in. Thus it seems like this chart doesn't apply. But a little reflection will show that it actually does because you can in fact assume that he raised the full amount that puts you all-in. You can make this assumption because if you do in fact play, that last $300 will be put in as well. If he did raise the full $1,000 you would be getting exactly 3-to-2 odds ($1,500-to-$1,000). Is that enough? Let's look at the chart. Against an average raiser the charts calls for pairs between aces and fives. So it looks like you should fold.

But let's not be too hasty. There are three reasons why you should seriously consider calling:

1. Your pot odds might be slightly greater than 3-to-2. Notice that if you were getting 2-to-1 you should call even with a pair of deuces.

2. He plays a bit looser than you thought. Notice if that he was in the loose category, a pair of deuces would again be a call.

3. Your stack has fallen below the threshold where you can afford to wait. We discussed this concept in another section and you are now indeed in that position. Thus you probably do need to make a stand with your pair of fours. Notice however that if it was the raiser and not you who was all-in, and you had a substantial stack, this consideration would not apply.

If we had changed the 4♦4♥ to the equally borderline

similar arguments would apply.

The above example was perhaps a bit trickier than a simple illustration of how to use this chart. But I'm sure you can handle it.

The Sklansky-Chubukov (S-C) Rankings

The sub-chapter above addressed calling all-in moves. Now we'll address making all-in moves.

A few years ago an article of mine appeared where I proposed the following problem. The blinds are $1 and $2. It is folded to you in the small blind. Your hand is ace-eight offsuit. And the big blind is a tough, tricky player. Notice that ace-eight is a difficult hand to play in no-limit hold 'em, especially out of position against a tough opponent. So perhaps the right play is to merely limp or maybe even to fold. But could that be right? After all, it is not often that the big blind will have a better hand than you.

Maybe moving in is best. Surely it's the right play if your stack or his stack is small. But what about if it is larger? Is there any way to come to a definitive answer?

After pondering this question for awhile I realized that there sort of was such a way. Simply put, it would be an easy matter to calculate whether a move-in would show a positive EV in comparison to folding, even if the opponent knew our hand. In other words, any stack size below a certain amount would have a better expected value than the negative $1 fold would, even if he saw my hand and played perfectly against it.

When I would poll people as to what they thought the maximum profitable move-in might be, their average answer was about 15 bucks. Almost everyone said something between $8 and $25. And they weren't close. The answer is about $70. As astonishing as this might seem, it really shouldn't be that surprising. There is $3 laying out there. If you move-in $70 you'll win that $3 the vast majority of the time (he can only call you with a pair or ace-eight or better). And when you do get called, you're about a 2-to-1 dog. I won't bore you with the math, but with a little reflection you should see that $70 makes perfect sense.

Now that's not to say that the right play is to move-in. All this calculation proves is that moving-in is better than folding, and only slightly better for that matter, as long as the stacks are higher than $40 or so. So in a tournament you might indeed avoid this move when you have a borderline situation.

On the other hand, notice something very important. This calculation assumes that your opponent knows your hand. In this case it means he will call you with ace-nine, or even ace-eight. And with that assumption, a $75 move-in would show a bigger loss than a fold.

But you and I both know that there is no way he will call such a big bet with ace-nine if he doesn't see your hand, nor for that matter ace-jack or a pair of fives. That being the case, raises much bigger than $70 would certainly still show a profit.

After working on this problem, it occurred to me that the same type of calculation could be made regarding any two cards in the small blind. In other words, given any two cards there was a maximum amount that could be successfully raised (by successful I mean it shows a better result than folding) even under the assumption that the big blind knows your hand and plays perfectly. But to do this calculation for every hand obviously requires a computer expert. So I went to our website at www.twoplustwo.com and tried to find one. And I did; Victor

Chubukov. A game theorist from UC Berkeley. This resulted in the "Sklansky-Chubukov (S-C) Rankings." Rankings that were checked and verified by others and are thus almost certainly accurate.

The following chart tells you the exact amount of chips you can profitably move-in with in the small $1 blind when the $2 big blind sees your cards and plays perfectly. With ace-eight offsuit that would be $70.96, with queen-five suited it would be $20.32, with four-deuce offsuit it would be $1.98, etc., etc.

The Sklansky -Chubukov Rankings (in Descending Order) of all 169 Hands	
Hand	Sklansky-Chubukov Number
AA	Inf
KK	953.9955
AKs	554.51
QQ	478.0082
AKo	331.8872
JJ	319.2136
AQs	274.2112
TT	239.821
AQo	192.6702
99	191.4139
AJs	183.2213
88	159.2969
ATs	138.9131
AJo	136.3105
77	134.8477
66	115.3485
ATo	106.2647
A9s	104.1248

55	98.62987
A8s	89.86565
KQs	86.6277
44	81.97959
A9o	81.7162
A7s	79.17591
KJs	72.62126
A5s	72.29213
A8o	70.95651
A6s	70.74453
A4s	66.65053
33	65.44082
KTs	62.80556
A7o	62.74775
A3s	62.27532
KQo	58.77166
A2s	58.14199
A5o	56.54209
A6o	56.15123
A4o	51.93949
KJo	50.83879
QJs	49.51544
A3o	48.44544
22	48.05412
K9s	47.81236

A2o	45.17234		Q3s	17.73401
KTo	44.94654		T8s	17.46571
QTs	43.80946		J7s	17.19452
K8s	39.91081		Q7o	17.07734
K7s	37.33065		Q2s	16.64103
JTs	36.10652		Q6o	16.29514
K9o	35.75415		98s	15.29334
K6s	34.89		Q5o	15.03498
QJo	32.81682		J8o	14.86776
Q9s	32.51971		T9o	14.83221
K5s	32.30333		J6s	14.7186
K8o	30.47389		T7s	14.19943
K4s	30.16328		J5s	14.04842
QTo	29.7164		Q4o	13.66217
K7o	28.54118		J4s	12.95547
K3s	28.38181		J7o	12.66604
K2s	26.73084		Q3o	12.50323
Q8s	26.71855		97s	12.25142
K6o	26.67571		T8o	12.15698
J9s	25.71252		J3s	12.04034
K5o	24.68097		T6s	11.92109
Q9o	23.41954		Q2o	11.30295
JTo	23.08525		J2s	11.13873
K4o	22.84502		87s	11.11055
Q7s	22.68524		J6o	10.78068
T9s	22.49148		98o	10.27126
Q6s	21.78516		T7o	10.20476
K3o	21.39222		96s	10.09767
J8s	20.63624		J5o	9.987293
Q5s	20.32186		T5s	9.9469
K2o	19.99942		T4s	9.260066
Q8o	19.81933		86s	8.994746
Q4s	18.91635		J4o	8.906238
J9o	17.79938		T6o	8.571955

97o	8.570963		53s	3.851054
T3s	8.415718		63s	3.777173
76s	8.318417		84o	3.737896
95s	8.261043		92o	3.585219
J3o	7.914721		43s	3.402163
T2s	7.538836		74o	3.366747
87o	7.505732		72s	3.221509
85s	7.239171		54o	3.221293
96o	7.074151		64o	3.170312
T5o	6.920957		52s	3.114999
J2o	6.885765		62s	3.054809
75s	6.59416		83o	2.994827
94s	6.583641		42s	2.796223
T4o	6.248512		82o	2.795837
65s	6.207388		73o	2.731972
86o	6.099835		53o	2.640274
93s	6.058991		63o	2.591343
84s	5.692773		32s	2.567461
95o	5.650827		43o	2.366073
T3o	5.480421		72o	2.243309
76o	5.439126		52o	2.181602
92s	5.359298		62o	2.139745
74s	5.109201		42o	1.976146
54s	4.850294		32o	1.825374
T2o	4.832254			
85o	4.81223			
64s	4.769221			
83s	4.463809			
94o	4.345783			
75o	4.269797			
82s	4.129509			
73s	4.018033			
93o	4.000304			
65o	3.972305			

So what's the best way to use this chart? That depends on what adjustments you need to make based on the situation. The simplest cases occur when you are indeed in the small blind, there is no ante, and you think your hand will play best if you can get all your money in immediately. The best example of these situations occur when you have a high card and a small card, especially unsuited. In these cases you really don't want to have to play post-flop out of position. On the other hand, you hate to just give up the blinds. It turns out that fairly significant move-ins will show a profit according to the S-C Rankings, and you should therefore usually make that move-in play.

This is doubly true because the numbers that the chart tells you are conservative. The real life numbers are higher still because in real life he will not be playing perfectly against you. Thus, again assuming the blinds are $1 and $2 and you are in the small blind, you should move-in $20 with queen-eight offsuit. In fact you should probably move-in with queen-seven offsuit or queen-trey suited, even though those rating are about 17 and 18 respectively. No reasonable player is going to be calling a $20 move-in with king-five, queen-eight, etc. And when you take those hands away from him your move-ins become profitable.

In fact, even a hand like ten-five suited can probably profitably move-in as much as $15, in spite of the S-C Ranking of approximately 10 because of the fact that the chart assumes your opponent will call with so many more hands than he actually will.

As your hands get better, more and more hands turn into profitable move-ins in the small blind. But that doesn't mean you should make that play. Remember that the numbers compare the EV of moving in to the EV of folding. Many hands will have a higher EV still if, instead of moving in, you make a small raise or a limp, (possibly followed by a fold if he raises). This is especially true if your hand plays well or if *you* play well. Hands like a pair of treys or queen-jack suited should ignore the S-C Rankings for the most part. $40 move-ins are better than folding, but almost certainly not better than a small raise or a limp. The exception would be if you are obviously not one of the better players at the table. If so, you should play an extremely aggressive pre-flop strategy.

Although this chart specifically covers the precise situation of the $1 small blind looking at a $2 big blind, it is easy to adjust to other situations. Suppose for instance there is an ante. Say the blinds are $100-$200, and there is a $25 ante. Again you are looking at ace-eight in the small blind. There would be very little error in finding your new answer through the use of pot odds. You know the right number is about $70 when the blinds are $1 and $2. Therefore you know that the S-C Rankings essentially allow you to lay up to about 23-to-1 odds, even when he knows your hand. So if you're playing with that ante in an eight handed game, laying 23-to-1 would mean you could move in up to $11,500 (as opposed to $6,900 if there was no ante). Since he doesn't see your hand, you could move-in even a bit more. See why super-aggressive pre-flop players often do well against those who have superior skills?

You can also use the S-C Rankings to estimate maximum move-in stacks when there is more than one person behind you. You won't be far off if you simply take the allowable odds that we talked about above, and divide by the number of players yet to act. So in the ace-eight case above (with an ante), a $5,750 move-in would be okay on the button. A $3,800 move-in would be okay in the cutoff seat. Again, I'm not suggesting that there are not better alternatives, especially if you are a good player. But if you know you've got your work cut out for you at the table you're at or you feel intimidated, let the S-C Rankings be your friend.

Sit 'n Go Tournaments

Sit 'n Go Tournaments are essentially one table satellites where there is more than one winner. Usually first prize is 50 percent of the total buy-in, second prize is 30 percent, and third prize is 20 percent. It turns out that the principles of tournament play apply even more to sit 'n go's than they do to a normal tournament: the gap concept, the importance of survival, first-in equity, waiting for others to go broke, and the fact that when you are in last place you must gamble if others are waiting for your demise.

The truth of the matter is that sit 'n go no-limit hold 'em tournaments are almost not really poker. None of the World Champions that you are used to seeing on TV would show a profit if they played the larger buy-in sit 'n go's available on Internet poker sites. Not unless they spent a good deal of time studying the often-times weird strategies that are required to play sit 'n go's expertly. These strategies are very technical and mathematical, and many hundreds of players have mastered them. I will not attempt to describe these strategies in detail, but I will give you a short overview of what I'm talking about. If you want to learn everything about sit 'n go's, you need to read *Sit 'n Go Strategy* by Collin Moshman and to visit the "Single Table Tournament (STT) Strategy Forum" at www.twoplustwo.com.

The main reason sit 'n go's are so different from cash games and even normal tournaments is that there is a giant jump in prize money from fourth to third. That jump (from 0 to 20 percent) is as great as the jump from second to first, and twice as much as from third to second. And whether you like it or not, that fact has great impact on the correct strategy.

For instance, suppose there are four players left, two have extremely small stacks, and your stack is just slightly smaller than the leader's. The chip leader goes all-in. The two tiny stacks fold, and it is up to you. If you fold, you are still almost certain to come in at least second, and will often win the tournament eventually. So let's say that if you fold your expected value is about 39 percent of the total buy-in. (Almost an even split between 30 and 50 percent.) If instead you play, and you lose, you come in fourth and get 0 percent. If you call and win, first is practically locked up, so we can say that your EV is about 49 percent of the total buy-in.

Well, let's look at this in terms of risk versus reward. When you fold you get 39 percent. If you call and win you move up to 49 percent, which is a 10 percent increase. But when you call and lose, you lose that 39 percent. So in essence, you are risking 39 percent to win 10 percent. That means you need to be about a 4-to-1 favorite to make the call. That pretty much limits you to aces and perhaps kings.

I'll have more to say about this in a moment. First, let's look at another example. Suppose there are four of you left, and all four of you have exactly equal chips. The other three players move-in before you. Notice that when the hand started, your EV is obviously 25 percent of the buy-in assuming you all play equally well. However, now that they have moved all-in, a simple fold on your part moves your EV up to 35 percent. (Do you see why?)

After the hand is over, you will have one-fourth of the chips, and you will be against one player who has three-quarters of the chips. You will win first place 25 percent of the time and second place 75 percent of the time, and the weighted average is 35 percent. If you chose to call your upside is 15 percent, since you go from 35 to 50 percent, but your downside is 18⅓ percent, since if you lose you will split the second and third prize with two other people, and get 16⅔ percent. For a call to be right you would have to think that you would win somewhat over 50 percent of the time since your risk is more than your reward. In a four-way pot, with everybody moving in, you are probably again talking only about aces and maybe kings.

But wait. To show you how tiny factors can change the correct play in a sit 'n go tournament, let's take the same situation except that you have one more chip than everyone else. This may not seem like a big deal, but it most certainly is. Because it means that if you call, and you lose, you get second place. Again, your expected value from folding is approximately 35 percent. So your risk in calling is only 5 percent. On the other hand, if you win this pot, you go from 35 percent to 50 percent, which means that you are now getting 3-to-1 odds in expected value, and should call with any hand that you think will win this four-way pot more than 25 percent of the time. Depending on how your opponents play, you can add quite a few more hands to the menu of good calls.

But now let's say you have $10 *less* than anyone else. Here we have a situation where your fold still results in approximately 35 percent of the prize money, and so your gain if you win is again 15 percent, but now your risk is that whole 35 percent since if you lose you get nothing. You are laying 35 percent to win 15 percent. You have to win this hand 70 percent of the time against three opponents to make the call right. In other words, you fold everything, including aces!

Now let's go back to that original problem where the chip leader forces you to fold all but aces and kings when there are two very short stacks. Since he knows that you are smart enough to realize the correct strategy, he should raise with any two cards. There is only a 1 percent chance that you can call him.

However, don't think that the fact that he has slightly more chips than you is that relevant. If he had slightly less chips it wouldn't change things much, not if your calling him would totally cripple you and allow the other two players a good chance at second and third.

In other words, there are many situations in sit 'n go's where the game becomes analogous to a game of chicken except that the first bettor has thrown his steering wheel out the window. It does not matter that the second guy knows what the first guy is doing. Unless he is suicidal he is forced to fold. Situations like this come up all the time in tournaments, but even more so in sit 'n go's. Again, I refer you to Collin Moshman's book and our website to gain a greater understanding of these situations.

The bottom line is that the concept of "first-in equity" is often extremely strong in the late stages of a sit 'n go tournament. And of course, the Gap Concept is highly related to the strength of first-in equity. The greater the importance of that equity, the bigger the gap between the raiser's requirements and the caller's requirements.

As to the importance of survival strategy notice that the giant prize for third place would lead one to such a strategy, especially in the early rounds. It is quite common for a player to sneak into third with less than his original buy-in. In fact, that player may have never had more than that buy-in at any time in the tournament. Clearly it is wrong to push small edges in a sit 'n go, especially if you are calling someone else's bet.

There is also another reason to play the initial stages quite tightly, especially when it comes to calling. It has to do with the fact that we are going to presume that you have, in fact, studied the detailed concepts related to the late stages of a sit 'n go, and most of your opponents have not. I have previously alluded to the mathematical fact that it is actually wrong to make big gambles with small edges if that risks being in a position to make similar gambles with bigger edges later on. The proper strategies late in a sit 'n go are so unusual compared to typical correct strategies that they afford those who know them a significant edge against even world champion players (in non-sit 'n go's). Thus it makes sense to wait until you get to that stage, if you know how to play it.

(Of course, if you are seriously playing sit 'n go's on the Internet, one after the other, perhaps multi-tabling, you may want to temper slightly your focus on survival. Reason being that plays which will very slightly lessen your EV will often also make the average amount of time that you spend on that sit 'n go decrease. So you might opt for that play since it will increase your hourly rate. In other words, better to play three sit 'n go's in two hours where each one earns you $40 on average than to earn $50 each on two sit 'n go's during the same two hours.)

Just to give you one other insight into the weird strategy of late stage sit 'n go's, I want to mention that we're not always just talking about being aggressive first-in, and super tight otherwise. For instance, the extreme importance of busting someone who is on the bubble will often lead you into making what appears to be timid plays. You might very well just limp in with a hand that you would normally raise with, or fold with for that matter, because you are trying to create a multiway pot that maximizes the chances that an all-in player will go broke. Elsewhere in this book I say that the common play of "checking it down" with an opponent when there is a third player all-in is usually a dumb thing to do. But it is much more likely to be correct when playing sit 'n go's, especially if the all-in player can bust one out of the money.

I have only scratched the surface regarding the intricate strategies of sit 'n go's, especially in the late stages. Hopefully, I've expounded enough so that you see you need to do some serious study if these tournaments are to become a major part of your poker income, and that you realize that you cannot expect to be successful at sit 'n go's without such study.

Additional No-Limit Hold 'em Hand Quizzes

1. Near the beginning of a tournament and everyone has plenty of chips. Your table is tough and will be broken up soon. The only bad player is in the big blind. You are under-the-gun with

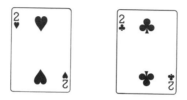

Call, raise, or fold?

> **Answer:** Normally, a pair of deuces in early position is a hand where all these plays are close. In this particular situation though the overriding factor is that there is a bad player in the big blind with plenty of chips. He might lose a lot more than a good player would if you make a set. Limp and hope to see a cheap flop.

2. $2,000 buy-in tournament. The money starts at $3,800 once the tournament is down to six tables. Average stack is $20,000. Three players need to be eliminated before the money is reached. You are in the cutoff seat with $31,000. Blinds are $300-$600 with a $50 ante. The button and both blinds all have about $10,000 in front of them. You are dealt:

What is your play?

Answer: Against typical opponents there is little doubt that the right play is to bring it in for almost exactly $2,500. It's a pure ante steal that needs to work two out of three times. But it will. Given the prize situation and the fact that the three players behind you will almost surely make the money if they don't get too rambunctious, we can assume they will play only about sevens or better, ace-king, or ace-queen. Of course, when they do have one of these hands they will probably move all-in and you will have to fold. But at least 75 percent of the time they will just give you the pot.

Note: Please read the next question as it elaborates on this one.

3. Same as the last one except this time you have

What is your play?

Answer: Obviously making it $2,500 to go would show a profit. After all if seven-deuce offsuit would, this hand will as well. The problem is that it would not show a greater profit. I say that because this size raise into these size stacks practically guarantees that any opponent will either fold or move in. And if they move in, you still have to fold.

Of course the problem with a smaller raise is that it won't win the pot nearly as often. If you raised to say $1,800 with either your 7♥2♣ or J♥9♥ your opponents would fold fewer hands. And while it is true that a smaller raise does not need to steal as often for it to be profitable, it is likely that a $2,500 bring-in wins undoubtedly quite a bit more often than an $1,800 bring-in. Making that play the higher EV from a pure ante steal standpoint.

Except the above assumes that the opponents move in or fold. Once you raise a smaller amount, somewhere between $1,500 and $1,800, it becomes reasonable for the other players to flat call that raise. Adding in this possibility changes the calculation. Your EV is now the instantaneous EV earn *plus* the money you make when the board comes down good for you. That total EV may be greater than the EV of making it $2,500 as a pure ante steal. And that total is obviously a bit higher with jack-nine suited than seven-deuce offsuit. Seven-deuce offsuit will almost never appreciate being merely called rather then reraised out. Jack-nine suited will. My play would be to open for $1,600.

4. $100-$200 blinds. No ante. You have the big blind and are dealt

Middle position makes it $600 to go. $400 to you. Your two options are to call or raise all-in. The all-in play is probably

the better one if your remaining chips (above the $400 call) are about how much?

> **Answer:** Roughly $600 to $5,000. With less than that the right play is the stop 'n go. (Just call and then bet the flop except possibly if an ace or king comes.) Above $5,000, you are probably better off calling and then waiting to see what comes.

5. Is there ever any reason to forego the stop 'n go play when you call a raise in the big blind and you have few reraising chips left?

> **Answer:** Not if you are heads up. Why would there be? Even if you have only one chip left, why not wait for the flop to bet it? Even if that will make him fold only one in a thousand times, it's better than nothing.
>
> But if the pot is three or more ways the situation changes. If you move in your remaining chips pre-flop, you will either thin the field (if someone can and does reraise) or you will get odds on your money. This is the right play multiway anytime you are in a situation where it is pretty clear you will be putting in the rest of your money regardless.

6. It is the beginning of a tournament. You are in the big blind with two aces. Several players limp in. How much should you raise?

> **Answer:** Probably not much. When stacks are deep, a moderate size raise in this situation is problematic. Especially when you do indeed have the hand your raise represents. It's likely to get one or two calls from players who are putting you on the right hand and have position on you. Not the best spot to be in.

A large raise is more likely to win the pot immediately, but with aces who wants that? On the other hand a mere check has drawbacks too. You disguise your hand but you also keep the pot so small as to make it very unlikely that you will win a lot of chips even when you flop a set. You also blow lots of money if one of the limpers was slowplaying with a hand he was planning to reraise with.

Thus I say that the right play can often be to raise a small amount, perhaps to three times the big blind, that will be called by everyone. They won't put you on aces so all you are really doing is tripling the stakes. Obviously this play has its downsides if you don't have the skill to play your hand right (including sometimes folding) when you don't flop a set. But that's not you is it?

7. $10,000 buy-in tournament. Half of the field is gone. You won a satellite and are honest enough with yourself to realize you are not as good as the other players at your table. You have average chips — $20,000. Blinds are $200-$400. You open for $1,200 in late position. The player on the button, who has you covered, calls. Your hand is

The flop is

You bet $1,800 and get called. The next card is the J♠. You check and your opponent checks. The last card is the 4♦. You check again and this time your opponent bets $3,000. What should you do?

> **Answer:** I believe the best play is to raise about $5,000. Although you probably have the best hand, your raise will make most good players throw away most, if not all, of the hands that beat you as well. The fact is that you played your hand exactly as you might have if you had a big flush. With no hand you would more likely come right out bluffing. With a good hand you would check and call. So he puts you on a monster.
>
> It's better to have the A♦ in your hand when you make this play since that eliminates your opponent having the nut flush. But even with that card the play is normally debatable except for the fact that your opponent is not only an excellent player, but is also doing his best to conserve chips in a tournament. You are being less careful because the table makeup and your skill level is forcing you to take chances.

8. $100-$200 blinds. You have put the big blind in and now have $1,200 left. All fold to the button who makes it $1,000 which is $800 to you after the small blind folds. You think he will make this play with any ace, king, pair, or two cards nine or higher. Your hand is

What now?

Answer: This is a question for our calling chart. First thing is to pretend that the raise is actually an amount that puts you all-in. Had he opened for $1,400 you would be getting $1,700-to-$1,200 odds. Since this is not quite 3-to-2, you need to be slightly tighter than the 3-to-2 section of the chart indicates.

Next, we need to see how loose this raiser is. Looking at the chart we can see he is somewhat tighter than how we define "very loose." That very loose player needs only two cards seven or higher whereas our opponent needs two cards nine or higher. So it looks like he's about halfway between "loose" and "very loose."

If we were getting 3-to-2 and he was very loose, the chart says that we have a clear call. Ten-seven suited and nine-eight suited make the chart. On the other hand, if your opponent was merely "loose," you would need, according to the chart, jack-ten suited. If you were getting only 6-to-5 instead of 3-to-2, you would need jack-nine suited even if he was "very loose."

Overall it looks like T♣9♣ just squeaks by. Whether you would play depends on the tournament situation. If you are a good player you should probably give up the tiny plus EV and fold.

Oh. One more point. Let's get back to that assumption that he actually made it $1,400 to go rather than $1,000. Since he really made it $1,000, the initial odds are not $1,700-to-$1,200, but rather $1,300-to-$800. Does that possibly swing things? Not really because the rest of the money will go in eventually the vast majority of the time. *But* that doesn't mean you should move in yourself. Remember the stop 'n go play. It probably won't work, but it can't hurt to try.

9. Blinds are $100-$200 in the middle of a tournament. Everyone folds to you in the small blind. You have a pretty short stack of $1,800 and hold the

The big blind has you easily covered. What's your play?

Answer: The Sklanksy-Chubukov Number is about $1,700. If he saw your hand, moving in would still be better than folding with that amount. This means that moving in $1,800 also has a greater EV than the minus $100 EV of folding since he will certainly fold many hands he wouldn't fold if he knew what you had.

But are there better options than moving-in? If your opponent is very weak, calling might be better since it could have as good as a break even EV. A small raise is out. With your stack size you can't easily fold to a reraise like you could if you only limp. So if you do raise it might as well be all-in to get him to fold pretty good hands.

But guess what? The answer could actually be to fold. That would be my play if I and the big blind were the two best players at the table. Here's why.

For one thing, if the big blind is an excellent player he won't be that far off on his calling hands if you move in. Secondly, if you limp he will often raise you out. Okay, but that doesn't change the fact that a move-in will still save a little EV.

But what about the fact that you are a big favorite at the table? And what about the fact that if you fold you have got lots of free hands coming up? These two future benefits override the small EV gain that you get by risking everything. Don't forget that if you do get called you will never be the favorite.

Hopefully this question gives you a bit more insight into how to use the Sklansky-Chubukov Charts when the situation is close.

10. $100-$200 blinds. Middle of a tournament. A good player brings it in for $600 in early position. You call with

The big blind pushes in his $3,000. The original raiser folds. You have him well covered. Should you call?

Answer: Here is another case for the calling chart. The chart mainly finds its best use when you are in the big blind because it assumes that there are no prospective callers behind you. But this is also the case here.

First, let's see what odds you are getting. There is $2,100 in the pot before the player in the big blind raises $2,400 (to $3,000). So you are getting $4,500-to-$2,400. A bit short of 2-to-1.

There is no reason to think that the big blind is totally desperate. Furthermore, he knows that it is reasonably likely he will get called. So it looks like this opponent will make this play with perhaps a pair of nines or better, ace-king, or ace-queen.

How convenient. That's exactly how the "tight" category is defined. And getting 2-to-1 you would call all the way down to jack-ten suited. Surely the slightly short price shouldn't swing things.

Think again. Even getting the full 2-to-1, king-queen suited is a fold! (It has to do with domination which is explained in more detail in *No-Limit Hold 'em: Theory and Practice*.) So you surely fold it here. Of course, if he was a smidgeon looser or your odds were at all higher you should probably gamble as long as you had plenty of chips left if you lost.

11. You are a good but not great player who has managed to get very close to the money. If you make the money, your $10,000 buy-in will turn into $20,000. After which the prize money will increase very slowly until the final table. The average stack is $60,000. You have $25,000. Four or five players are below $10,000. Two of them need to bust out for you to cash.

The blinds are $500 and $1,000 with a $100 ante. A world class multiple bracelet winner is on your right. His stack is also $25,000. He opens in middle position for $2,500. You call on his immediate left with

Everyone else folds. The flop comes:

He bets $3,000. What is your play?

Answer: Normally the typical tournament play is to just call given the bubble situation described. To risk all of your chips with a raise is almost always contraindicated if the alternative play is reasonable and it greatly increases your chances of significantly increasing your prize money.

On the other hand, I have been emphasizing that if you are faced with better players you should not box with them but should instead go for the knockout punch. And that is doubly true if you know that they are also trying to survive. That argues for a move-in on your part.

In this case though that play isn't as good as it seems because your opponent is not desperate for money. And even if he doesn't realize that you are employing a strategy of putting pressure on the best players, he will probably call you with aces, ace-king, or king-queen (plus king-king of course) and it is likely he has one of these hands. He will think a while before he calls, but he will call.

That doesn't mean that your moving-in with the A♦Q♦ is a bad play. It just means that it is close. And to make this close play hurts your EV when you are two out of the money.

On the other hand, if this tournament is all about winning or at least getting into the top three, then go ahead and push those chips in. You will get no argument from me.

12. You are a world class player. You are in a $10,000 buy-in event with a surprisingly weak field. Unfortunately, you just lost a key pot where you called someone else's all-in bet and he drew out on you. You are down to $1,400 playing a $100-$200 blind with a $25 ante. The player under-the-gun makes it $600 to go and you are next. You have

at an eight handed table. What is your play?

Answer: First, I want to note that no good player should ever let himself get this low if he can help it. See the *Harrington On Hold 'em* books for more details. But this couldn't be helped.

In this situation the only two alternatives are obviously to fold or move-in. And while a move-in will probably knock out everybody behind you, the opener will certainly call.

So in essence you will probably be in a situation, if you move-in, where you are getting $1,900-$1,400 odds. Although the calling chart was not devised for this situation, it still works well. And the chart tells us that ace-jack offsuit barely makes it if your opponent could have aces down through sevens, ace-king down through ace-ten, or king-queen and you are getting 3-to-2 odds.

Neither is the case here. So it seems even an average player should fold. Since you are a world class player who is avoiding close gambles for all your chips you might assume the fold is clear cut.

But you would be wrong. The overriding consideration is the desperateness of your situation. You are anteing $25 every hand and the blinds are coming up. You don't have enough time, or the chips, to wait for a hand where your skill matters. Pushing here is slightly negative EV. But not pushing is worse yet.

Additional
No-Limit Hold 'em Concepts

Afterthought

Again, it's difficult for someone like myself who has been around for a long time to accept the fact that no-limit hold 'em is now so popular. Yes, I'm aware of the TV shows that first appeared in 2003 that caught everyone's interest because the hole cards were shown and a whole new (and much larger) generation of poker players quickly appeared. And I'm also aware of the contribution that the Internet made to our game in spreading its popularity. But it's still hard to believe that no-limit hold 'em, and no-limit hold 'em tournaments are so popular.

You need to understand that it wasn't too many years ago that no-limit hold 'em ring games were few and far between. Thus when a no-limit hold 'em tournament was offered, many players would pass since this was a game they were unfamiliar with. Only the hard core tournament players wanted to play no-limit, partly because they understood its strategy better, and the fields were much smaller.

Today, all that has changed. And some events only offer no-limit tournaments. So adding this section was absolutely essential. It was fun to write, and I hope you picked up a few things.

Part Six

Questions and Answers
by Mason Malmuth

Questions and Answers

Introduction

David has covered a great deal of material in this book. However, for many people, reading and learning can be two different things. Consequently, to help you retain some of the more significant ideas, I have reiterated them in a question-and-answer format.

I suggest that, after you have read and studied the text, try to answer the following questions. You probably will want to go over them many times. In addition, I suggest that you cover the answer that immediately follows each question. Only look at the solution after you have answered the question to the best of your ability.

Also, it needs to be pointed out that what follows is not a substitute for the text. In fact, some of the ideas in the text are not contained here. But enough material is included so that after you have thoroughly digested the text, the questions should help keep your tournament poker sharp.

Finally, the questions and answers are organized by topics covered in the text, so you can easily return to the appropriate section for a fuller explanation.

EV

1. What does expected value mean?

   The amount you will average winning or losing, per bet, if you could somehow make it a large number of times.

2. Why is it not always right to choose the play with the highest EV?

   Because the higher EV bet may be more likely to lose.

3. What if you have enough money to withstand short-term fluctuations?

   In that case it is always better to choose the bet with the higher EV.

4. What if you do not have that cushion?

   It may well be right to choose the slightly smaller EV if that bet will win more often.

5. When is this especially true?

   If going broke keeps you from making lots more positive EV bets.

6. What is a major factor involving EV in proper tournament strategy?

   Balancing your quest for extra EV and your quest for survival.

You're Broke
— You're Done

1. How does the way tournaments are typically paid influence your strategy?
   You should avoid close gambles with a slight advantage.

2. When does this take on most significance?
   Near the end of a tournament.

3. What is another reason to eschew close gambles even early on?
   If you are one of the best players in the tournament.

4. When can it be mathematically correct to pass up a mathematically good bet?
   If losing that bet can keep you from making an even better bet later on.

5. What if you have a heads-up situation with a hand that is only barely worth playing, EV wise?
   You seriously consider folding if losing that pot would get you broke or nearly broke.

6. What if you have a decision to slowplay a good hand?
   Assuming you are one of the best players in the tournament, many prospective slowplays should not be made.

7. When does this principle apply?
   Only on close decisions.

8. When do you gain a lot from deception?

Anytime you can deceive your opponents at lower stakes to the point where they will make a mistake against you once the stakes are raised.

9. What if your risk is small?

The idea of avoiding close gambles doesn't apply.

10. Example?

Seeing the flop with 3♥3♦ getting debatable odds.

11. What can you expect if you have the smallest stack at the last table?

Most of your opponents will be playing conservatively, hoping you go broke.

12. What should you do?

You must take chances and hope to get lucky.

13. What if other small stacks are foolishly playing too loosely?

The above strategy totally reverses.

14. Do the concepts in the chapter apply when you are thinking of betting or opening?

Not always. You will not play *fewer* hands (when first in) than you would in a normal game, but in fact, most likely play *more*. The avoidance of close gambles applies only to calling or betting in spots where you know you will be called.

15. What are two common situations where your tournament skills may be lacking?

When you are relatively new to tournaments or when you're at a tough table that won't be broken for a while.

16. What do you do when this is the case?

Embrace those close gambles and take a few chances.

They're Broke
— They're Done

1. What is quite common to see in a tournament?
   A player who is notorious for his looseness in normal games playing significantly tighter when he has a small or moderate stack.

2. What do you need to notice about your opponents?
   How tightly they are playing and play accordingly.

3. What do the most successful tournament players do?
   They aggressively go after small pots and quickly back off at the first sign of strength from their opponents.

The Gap Concept

1. What important first round principle is understood by all good poker players?

    You need a better hand to play against someone who has already opened the betting than you would need to open yourself.

2. What is the "Gap?"

    The difference between the hand you need to call (or raise) an opener with and that with which you would open yourself.

3. What does the width of the gap depend on?

    How tight your opponents play.

4. What if your opponents are quite loose?

    There may be no gap at all.

5. What about in a tournament?

    The gap is often extremely high.

6. What should you do differently than usual?

    In a tournament, it is often right to open raise with hands far inferior to those which you would need to call.

7. Hold 'em examples?

    If three people fold, you should probably raise with Q♣J♦ or 5♠5♥.

8. What if the under-the-gun player has raised, you are next, and you hold A♦K♥?

    Consider folding it.

9. When playing stud, what if you have the highest card showing (not duplicated elsewhere) and no one, except the bring-in, has entered the pot?

You should usually raise.

10. What if someone else raises in front of you?

You should usually fold any pair lower than the denomination of the upcard that had raised.

11. What about drawing hands?

Be less apt to play hands such as J♥8♥5♥ or three straights.

12. What if the players behind you have either a very small or very large stack?

Loosening up on your normal opening requirements may be unwise because you are less likely to steal from them.

13. What are exceptions to the Gap Concept (where someone else has opened)?

If the raiser in front of you has a lot of chips, or if he is not worried about going broke, *or* if he is aware of the Gap Concept.

Prize Structure Implications

1. What are you rooting for at the last table?
   For someone else to go broke.

2. What is bad to do late in a tournament?
   To risk large sums on near break even situations.

3. But what if you have a half decent edge?
   It could still be wrong to gamble.

4. What if you are the one who makes the first bet?
   By being the "aggressor," you find yourself more likely than usual to win small pots.

5. What is the bottom line here?
   The Gap Concept becomes even stronger when players are in the money or close to it.

6. What should you do when against players who are aware of the disadvantage of fighting close decisions when others gain by watching?
   You can aggressively steal small pots, even if they suspect that this is what you are doing.

7. What if it is the other player who raises?
   You need an even better hand than usual to play.

When They Call You

1. What two facts have a significant impact on your later round play, especially the second round?

    You are raising with *more* starting hands than you might normally be used to, and that they are calling your raises with *fewer* hands.

2. What if your hand is quite good?

    Be prepared to sandbag more than usual.

3. Stud example?

    You raise with 7♣K♦K♥ and are called by ? ? Q♠. Since he is more likely than usual to have queens, you should try for a check raise on fourth or fifth street.

4. Limit hold 'em example?

    You raise with A♦A♣. The flop is Q♣3♠2♥. You bet (the flop) and get called. You should go for a check raise on fourth street.

5. What if your hand is merely good?

    You should often immediately go into a check calling mode.

6. Limit hold 'em example?

    You raise with A♦J♦, get called, and the flop is A♣T♠4♥. Proper tournament strategy is to frequently go into a defensive shell and just check and call.

7. What if your hand is worse than usual?

    Be prepared to "be done with it" on the next round.

8. Why is firing at least "one more barrel" usually not right in a tournament with a weak hand?

You must take into consideration the necessity of conserving chips, the fact that you are up against a better hand than usual, and the fact that your hand is not as good as it normally would be.

9. What is an important exception to the above regarding hold 'em and Omaha high-low-split eight-or-better?

When ragged small cards come in hold 'em, or big cards in Omaha high-low-split eight-or-better. In that case, you can bet a weak hand twice.

10. Hold 'em example?

You raise with Q♣J♥ and get called. It is probably worth taking a shot at the pot when the flop is 8♣6♠4♥.

11. What play can you sometimes make, particularly in a no-limit tournament, that's the opposite of what has been discussed?

You might call a raise from a very weak player if you're behind him in late position. Then on the flop, if your opponent checks and your hand is weak, a bet will often steal it.

12. Why is this play better in no-limit?

A weak playing opponent will be afraid to get involved in a situation where his hand is questionable.

Chips Change Value

1. How does the value of each individual chip that you win compare to the previous ones?

   They are worth less.

2. What is the bottom line?

   With few exceptions, what you gain by winning a chip is not quite as much as what you lose when you lose a chip.

Keeping the Pot Small

1. What does an extra raise on your part do?
   It changes the nature of the whole hand from that point forward.

2. What does a bigger pot do?
   It causes everyone to stay in longer.

3. How does that affect you?
   You might have to take cards off that you would not have had to, had the pot been smaller.

4. What are the implications of bigger pots?
   Your opponents will chase more often when you have the best hand and might win a pot that you would have otherwise won.

5. What if the game is no-limit?
   This idea does not hold if everyone has plenty of chips since your future bets can be sized to control the odds you are offering your opponent.

6. What's another reason to keep the pots small?
   Opponents' hands are easier to read.

The First Level

1. In the larger tournaments are your results at the first level important?

No. They are almost inconsequential to your eventual chances of winning.

2. What does this mean?

You may want to consider playing a much looser style than you will in succeeding levels.

3. What is the reason for this?

You are trying to create an impression that you can take advantage of when the stakes rise.

4. What do you do at the succeeding levels?

During the second and third level you revert to tighter play, while from the fourth level on you would typically continue to play tight, but make more frequent aggressive stabs at stealable pots.

Limping

1. In a limit hold 'em tournament how often should you limp when no one else is in?
   Rarely.

2. Why?
   There is simply too great a chance that you will steal the blinds if you raise. Meanwhile, multiway pots are much rarer in tournaments which gives you less reason to limp with hands that prefer them.

3. Examples?
   Hands like Q♠J♠ or 7♣7♦ under-the-gun, if played at all, should usually be brought in with a raise.

4. What about no-limit and the stacks are deep?
   Limping or small raises can be correct if they have the potential of allowing you to make a big hand that might trap your opponent for a lot of chips.

5. What if the stakes have increased to the point where many of the stacks are in jeopardy?
   Revert to the more standard raise, if first in, strategy.

6. What about when playing seven-card stud?
   You still limp fairly often.

7. Why?
   Since one of your cards is showing, you cannot as easily represent a powerful hand when your upcard is small.

8. Example?

You have a live three flush, with a small card showing, such as J♥8♥4♥.

9. What if your three flush was with a high upcard?

We revert back to the Gap Concept and will raise more than we would in a side game.

10. In hold 'em, what if someone limps in in front of you?

You must tighten up as opposed to being first in.

11. Be specific?

If your hand is merely good, you should be more apt to simply limp behind them rather than raise.

12. Example?

If a good player limps in first position usually fold K♥Q♦ (but call if the hand was suited) and call with A♣Q♥.

13. Stud example?

If a small card limps, don't raise without a big pair.

14. What about no-limit hold 'em?

It is different. The best players should be doing a lot of limping even with mediocre hands.

15. Why?

The Gap Concept doesn't apply in the early rounds of no-limit where the stack size is great compared to the blinds.

When Will
Your Table Break Up?

1. If your table will break up soon, what obvious effect on your strategy does it have?

   You make no "advertising" plays.

2. What if your table is scheduled to break up soon, and you are playing against much tougher opponents than the average player in the rest of the room?

   Stay away from close gambles.

3. What if you find yourself at a tough table that will not break up for quite awhile?

   You can't play extra tightly in the hopes of conserving your chips for a different table.

4. What if you will have to play at a table for a long time?

   Setting up plays for the future is even more important than in regular side games because the play you set up will most likely be at bigger stakes.

Adjusting Strategy
Because the Stakes Rise

1. What if it is near the end of a tournament, you have a small stack, and the stakes will soon rise?
> You should avoid taking risks in marginal situations at the lower limit.

2. Why?
> There is a better chance you will be able to sneak into a higher money position at the higher stakes when the stacks that are slightly ahead of you are apt to bust out.

3. What is the biggest reason to change your strategy as a result of subsequent increases in stakes?
> The payoffs from creating an impression early are greater than they would be in a normal ring game.

4. What if you play somewhat aggressively or wildly early on?
> This results in getting calls down the road that you otherwise might not have gotten.

5. Why does this strategy pay off more in tournaments than it does in a normal game?
> Because those calls will be at bigger stakes.

6. What is an alternate strategy?
> To play very tightly, and even timidly early on, in order to set up a bluff down the road.

7. Which of these two alternate strategies should you use?
> As a general rule, use the first strategy in no-limit or pot-limit tournaments, and the second strategy in limit tournaments.

Noticing the Short Stacks

1. What typically happens to players with much less than the average amount of chips in front of them?
    They are ready to give up.

2. What does this mean?
    It is often unwise to make your usual semi-bluff thrust at a small pot.

3. What is another reason to notice whether you might be up against a short stack?
    So that you can adjust your hand selection towards starting hands that do well "hot and cold."

4. To what game does this concept mainly apply?
    Hold 'em, especially no-limit hold 'em.

5. Example?
    J♠T♠ is normally much better than A♣9♦, but not if you are running the cards out against the kind of hands (such as king-ten or king-nine) that a desperate short stack might call you with.

6. Should you make sub-optimal plays simply because they might help eliminate a short stack?
    Almost never.

Noticing the Large Stacks

1. Are players with large stacks afraid of going broke?
   Most are not.

2. What are the implications?
   They are likely to call you with mediocre holdings or initiate the betting with such holdings.

3. How, in general, does it affect your play?
   You need to loosen up slightly when they open the pot, and tighten up slightly when they are behind you and you are considering opening.

4. What else is important to realize?
   Some players with a large stack are a little more prone to play their hands in a tricky manner.

5. What does this mean?
   Against a player like this you'll need to be a little more cautious than normal.

When the
Blinds are Coming Up

1. There is one hand to go before your blind, and you have only enough chips to put in that blind when it comes to you. What should you do?

Play hands worse than you would normally play, but not merely better than average.

2. What if there is more than one hand to go before you are forced to put in the blind or your final ante?

The degree you loosen up would be even less.

3. What if you can wait four or five hands?

There should be almost no change in your strategy compared to normal (unless there is a significant ante).

All-In Strategy

1. What is one of the major differences between regular poker games and tournament poker?
   In tournaments, a player is often all-in.

2. Should you start playing poor hands when your stack is short?
   No.

3. If you are in the big blind, and all you have left is enough to call a raise, and a player is raising pre-flop either in the dark, or is in a strategic situation where he will raise with just about anything, what should you do playing limit hold 'em?
   Call no matter what you have.

4. When is the decision more ticklish?
   You have more than enough to call or it is a no-limit hand where his raise gives you less than 3-to-1 odds to call. Or, the hand you are facing is to varying degrees better than random.

5. What if you are playing no-limit?
   The size of your opponent's raise now becomes very relevant.

6. What does that mean?
   Even if you think he will raise with anything, you should still throw away your worst hands when his raise will put you all-in and give you odds of 2-to-1 or worse.

7. Suppose you have some inkling about what type of hands your opponent will raise you with?
   You can, in theory, calculate which hands to call with based on his possible holdings and the odds you are getting.

8. In hold 'em, what are the effects of future betting?
   Certain hands go down or up in value.

9. Examples?
   A sometimes playable hand like 8♠6♠ is rarely worth playing all-in, whereas a usually unplayable hand like A♥9♣ or K♥T♣ may well be worth moving in with, even though they should usually be folded if more chips are at risk later.

10. What is an exception with a hand like 8♠6♠?
    It is when you can get 2-to-1 on your money but only be against one player.

11. Example?
    There is a raise and a move-in. The player all-in has a lot of chips and the initial raise was about the size of your stack. If the player who went all-in would still have a wide range of hands, and the initial raiser is now likely to fold, especially if you call, you will be getting a little better than 2-to-1 on your call.

12. In seven-card stud, if an all-in pot seems imminent, how does it affect hand values?
    Small and medium pairs go up in value, while small three flushes and three straights go down.

13. Examples?
    You might play a hand like 5♥9♦5♠ but throw away a hand like 5♥9♥3♥.

14. Omaha high-low-split eight-or-better example?
    A♣K♠J♥4♦ is probably worth playing all-in, even in spots where it would normally be folded.

Just Out of the Money

1. If you are one of the short stacks, should you alter your play to try to sneak into the money?

If you are only concerned with maximizing your EV, you should.

2. What if you choose to make no adjustments?

You will much more often come in one out of the money, but occasionally reach one of the higher prizes.

3. What can you do if you are concerned about getting into the money?

Check the other tables and notice how your stack compares to everyone else's.

4. What if your stack is bigger than the stacks of one or two players at the other tables?

Assuming we are talking about stacks that are so small that losing one hand will deplete it, you should stay away from all close gambles and maybe even some not so close.

5. When can the "gap" get very large?

Right before the money where the initial prizes, while a small part of the total pool, can seem large in absolute terms to some players.

7. What does this mean?

If no one is yet in, it can become correct to raise with some very questionable hands. But if someone else has already raised, especially if it appears to be a player who is very concerned about making the money, your range of playable hands should now be greatly reduced.

Just In The Money

1. What happens to some of your opponents after they make the money?

    They won't care anymore since they have now made the money.

2. What does this mean?

    They'll play exceptionally loose.

3. When is this especially true?

    If the next few places all pay the same amount.

A Special Last
Two Table Situation

1. What will the short stacks do when the combination of the two tables is imminent (and the main money is at the final table)?
   They will tend to throw away all but their very best hands.

2. What should the chip leader at the table do?
   Raise with an awful lot of hands.

3. What about the player with the second largest stack?
   He is in a similar position, provided that the largest stack has already folded.

4. Suppose the shortest stack raises almost all-in. What should the chip leader do if he holds a hand like Q♥Q♣?
   He should consider folding.

5. Why?
   The gain from playing this hand might not be worth having the tables combined and no longer being able to run over the game.

The Last Table

1. What is mandatory to take into account if you make the last table?

   The amount of money involved in moving up a place or two can be significantly more than the face value of the chips.

2. To whom do the strategy adjustments designed to move you up in standings apply?

   The players with fairly short stacks.

3. What if you have a moderate stack?

   You should make few adjustments.

4. Example?

   If there are nine players left, you have an average amount of chips, are in about fifth place, you could almost certainly ante your way into sixth prize. But given the increase in prizes paid to the last three places that are typical in most tournaments, any strategy along those lines would be ridiculous.

5. What is the major exception?

   When playing no-limit, and you are facing a stack that can bust you.

6. What is the basic idea when you are in next to last place?

   If you are in next to last place, but still quite short, you should tend to go out of your way to avoid going broke before the shorter stack does.

7. What if you have the smallest stack?
   The situation is the opposite. You should usually gamble, or at least not play any tighter than normal.

8. Why?
   Because it is likely that the player who has the second smallest stack is waiting for you to go broke.

9. What if the player with a slightly larger stack is disregarding you and still taking chances?
   Play extra tightly, and hope to sneak ahead of him.

10. Example?
    In limit hold 'em, fold Q♣J♥ if you're one to the right of the button with the second smallest stack.

11. But what if the smallest stack doubles up?
    The Q♣J♥ becomes a raising hand first in, especially if your recent play was very tight.

Down to Two Players

1. What's important?
   That you don't relax.

2. Why might you want to make a deal?
   By the time it is heads-up, losing two or three pots in a row that go all the way to the river will certainly eliminate the shorter stack.

3. If you don't make a deal, should you change your strategy from typical heads-up games?
   It depends on your skill level compared to your opponent's.

4. What if he is better than you?
   You must be aggressive.

5. What if you're the better player?
   Play your normal game, except you should try to avoid playing big pots with close decisions.

6. What is the only major mistake you could make heads-up?
   To play so tightly that you are destined to be ground down from ante steals.

Rebuy Tournaments

1. In tournaments where most people tend to rebuy if they go broke, what should your strategy be during the rebuy period?
   It should somewhat revert back to what you would use in normal games.

2. How do most players in a rebuy tournament play before their rebuy option expires?
   Significantly looser.

3. How does this affect your strategy?
   It shrinks the "Gap" in your opening versus calling requirements.

4. Should you rebuy if you are one of the better players in the tournament?
   Yes.

5. Should you add-on?
   It depends on how well you are doing.

6. What is a conservative rule of thumb regarding proportional add-ons?
   To add-on if you have less than the average number of chips at that point (after you include the others' add-ons), and not otherwise.

7. What if the tournament allows add-ons far in excess of the original buy-in?
   If you can afford it, and are one of the best players, you must seriously consider making this add-on, even if you are already doing well.

8. What if the tournament charges less per chip for your add-on than they do for your original buy-in?

You must almost always opt to purchase these cheaper chips.

Satellites

1. What is the proper strategy for a one table satellite?
   Somewhere between the proper strategy for a regular tournament and a side game.

2. When there is only one winner, how should you play in theory?
   Exactly as if you were playing in a normal game.

3. But what about in practice?
   You still have to worry about the fact that you cannot buy more chips.

4. What does this mean?
   You should avoid gambling in very close situations if you are a better player than most of your opponents.

5. Can you take advantage of the fact that your opponents are afraid of going broke?
   Many players don't worry about it. So you have to identify those who do. Then you will know who to apply the Gap Concept against and which ones not to.

6. What about super satellites?
   They are almost exactly the same as normal tournaments.

7. What if there are several winners, all of whom get the same prize?
   This forces you to sometimes play even tighter than in a normal tournament.

Making Deals

1. How much does playing superiority count for regarding deals?
   Very little due to the size of the stakes compared to the stacks.

2. What is the exception?
   If your opponent folds too much.

3. When calculating the fair price of a deal, why can you not be precise when there are three players?
   There is no ironclad way to calculate the chances of coming in second and third based on your chip position.

4. What happens in most three-way settlements?
   The third guy tends to shortchange himself.

5. What's the best time to take advantage of this misunderstanding?
   When you are the chip leader, or close to it, in a three-or four-way finish, especially if the shorter stacks are small, but not tiny.

Some No-Limit Observations

1. What tournaments are most profitable for the best players?
   No-limit hold 'em tournaments.

2. When does the Gap Concept apply to these no-limit tournaments?
   To larger opening bets or later rounds.

3. What if the opening bet is small?
   If you are one of the better players, you can play a lot of hands that are cheap to come in with because of the edges you can obtain from future bets.

4. What about marginal confrontations against good players with larger stacks?
   It is more important to avoid these confrontations in no-limit than it is in limit.

5. What about playing against small stacks who are trying to survive?
   They are easier to take advantage of since they know you can bust them in one hand.

6. What about your knowledge of all-in prices?
   It is rewarded much more in no-limit than in a limit game since all-in situations and decisions as to whether to call all-in, or raise someone else all-in, come up much more often.

7. When does it hurt the most when someone makes a big bet or raise into us?
   When we have a close decision as far as calling or not is concerned.

8. What if we know that we probably have a better hand than they do when they make that bet or raise.

We welcome the action.

9. What if their bet or raise indicates that we have no chance of having the best hand or drawing out?

That bet or raise does not hurt, since we fold.

10. How does it affect things when someone forces us to call when we are probably beaten or forces us to fold when we still had a chance?

It's very bad, especially in no-limit where a person can bet or raise an amount that puts maximum pressure on us.

11. What dose this mean?

With such hands we should usually avoid raising, check raising, or betting in last position since that will open up the possibility of getting reraised.

12. What is a common mistake made by beginning no-limit players?

To put in fairly big bets or raises before the flop with hands that are very good, but not so good as to welcome a reraise.

13. Examples?

Hands like T♦T♥ or A♥Q♥ with lots of chips in front of you.

14. What are the three reasons that ace-king prefers to be all-in before the flop in a no-limit game?

1. It will sometimes be the best hand, even without improving, when all the cards are out.
2. Most of the time that ace-king wins it is with one pair — a hand that is very tricky to play.
3. A large percentage of the time that ace-king wins a showdown it will be when it caught an ace or a king on

fourth or fifth street. If it is not all-in, it will often not be around to catch those cards.

15. What is important to understand about ace-king?
It is a lot better to be the bettor when you put all your money in rather than calling someone else's all-in bet.

16. What about ace-queen?
It is quite a bit worse off than ace-king if one of the opponent's possible calling hands is ace-king. It is also twice as likely to run into a pair of kings.

17. When is the best time to move in with ace-king?
When moving in is betting two to five times the size of the pot.

18. What if the bet is smaller than this?
You will usually get called, especially when someone else has already bet.

19. What about raising or betting more than five times the size of the pot?
That is also debatable because you might be risking too much to win too little.

20. So what should you do if you have significantly more than five times the pot and hold ace-king?
You may decide that it is better to just call or perhaps raise a small enough amount that you can fold if reraised.

21. How can you negate most of a better player's edge?
By getting all-in before the flop.

Don't Worry About the "Average Stack"

1. Should you make an effort to keep up with the average stack?
   No.

2. When is this a definite mistake?
   If it results in your playing your below average stack the same as a short stack.

3. When is your stack considered short?
   If it is below 15 big blinds — a bit more if there is an ante.

4. What *should* you worry about?
   The size of the blinds and the ante.

Focus on
the Weaker Opponents

1. What if you and your opponents each have a large stack?
   Lean towards confrontations with bad players, and away from confrontations with good players.

2. When does this usually occur?
   At the beginning of the event or later on if you have built up your chips and there happens to be some bad players at your table who have gotten lucky.

3. What strategy should you use against a timid player?
   Tend to bluff him.

4. How about against a non-bluffer?
   Tend to save money.

5. How about against a wild player?
   Seek high implied odds.

6. What if you are at a table that won't break for a long time?
   Loosen up against the bad players, but also *tighten* up against the good players, especially those with large stacks.

7. What if all the live players are gone or on short stacks?
   Switch gears and confront the tough players head on.

Focus on the Short Stacks

1. If your opponent has a lot of chips and plays well, what should you avoid doing?

> You should not play close decisions against him if you have a lot of chips as well.

2. What if he has a short stack?

> You should no longer avoid gambling with only a little bit the best of it.

3. What if the short stack is owned by a bad player?

> It is better yet.

4. Why?

> If you double him up, you have a better chance of getting it all back.

When the
Big Blind is Short or Weak

1. What if the player in the big blind doesn't have very many chips or doesn't play very well?
   You should play a few more hands.

2. Why is folding hands like ace-queen, ace-jack, king-queen, or king-jack a mistake when the big blind is short stacked?
   You won't be facing big bets on the later streets.

3. What if your opponent is a bad player, especially if he is timid?
   We can assume he won't bet lots of chips unless he has one pair beaten.

4. What else may happen with a bad player?
   We can often get him to pay off larger bets with our one pair hand than a better player would.

5. What about the players behind you?
   This is usually not that big a problem.

6. Why?
   If the big blind is on a short stack there will often be all-in situations with a little or no side pot. When this occurs, even good players are not apt to try to bet you off your big pair.

7. How about when the big blind is a bad player?
   The situation is similar. The pot is now protected.

8. How should you play aces or kings if you are in very late position, no one else is in, and the big blind is weak-tight?
   Just call.

When the
Antes are All You Need

1.What if you are at a table with players so tight that mere ante stealing can show a profit, or at least keep you close to even?

It is imperative that you recognize this situation, take advantage of it, and in many cases adjust your post-flop play as well.

2. When do you typically find tables like this?

At or about the time the ante is first introduced.

3. When your table has this characteristic, that is you can frequently steal the antes, how does this affect the other hands you play?

You should play other hands much more carefully.

Implication of the Modern Tournament Prize Structure

1. What is the modern prize structure?

    It is when about 10 percent of the field is paid approximately twice the buy-in, but very little more until you reach the top 1 percent or so.

2. What if you are near the bubble and gamble all your chips with a slight edge?

    You are hurting yourself EV wise.

3. What happens as your stack gets smaller?

    Then this is even more true (unless your stack is so tiny that you have little chance of reaching the money without winning a pot).

The Stop 'n Go Play

1. What is the Stop 'n Go Play?
   If your chip stack is such that moving in pre-flop will virtually always get called, you can call before the flop and then move in on the flop.

2. When is this the better play?
   Those times your hand is not that strong.

3. How strong?
   Strong enough to make your call of his raise correct.

4. What does this play do for you?
   It allows you to increase your EV versus going all-in before the flop.

5. Example?
   The blinds are $100 and $200, the ante is $25, and the table is eight handed. You are in the big blind with 2♣2♦ and have $1,000 behind. The button makes it $600 to go and you know he will do this with any two cards. The small blind folds. Your play is to just call the $400 raise and then bet $600 on the flop, except possibly if a deuce comes.

6. What if you had eights instead of deuces in this example?
   Then it is almost definitely better to move in pre-flop.

Some Unusual
Plays with Aces and Kings

1. What should you not overly fear when you have aces or kings?
   Getting drawn out on if you don't raise people out pre-flop.

2. What usually happens when your kings are beaten?
   An ace comes on board and you lose a lot less than when your aces are beaten.

3. If you raise before the flop with two aces (or possibly two kings) and an opponent reraises, what should you do?
   Consider flat calling, especially if it is heads-up.

4. What if you reraise?
   You have pretty much given your hand away and your opponent will often fold immediately.

5. Suppose it is the beginning of a tournament, someone in early position opens for a typical raise, three to five times the big blind, and you are in early position behind him with a pair of kings, should you reraise?
   At most tables, reraising is wrong.

6. What might happen if you make this play?
   A pretty good hand behind you that would have folded had you raised, might now raise themselves. If the original raiser just calls, you can make a big reraise.

7. What's another reason to make this play?
   It is easily possible the original raiser has two aces.

8. If you are at a table that is aggressive, what may be worth doing?

To limp in with aces and kings, even in fairly late position,

9. What is necessary for this play to be correct?

That the stacks be large relative to the blinds and antes, and some of the players behind you be greedy.

•

Snapping Off All-In Moves

1. What are many players aware of today?
   The value of first-in, all-in, pre-flop bets with a moderately short stack.

2. What is the net result of this?
   It doesn't take that good a hand to be a favorite over the average hand players in this situation will push with.

3. What are some hands you can consider calling with?
   Ace-jack, king-queen, a pair of sevens, or possibly even slightly worse.

4. What if there are many players yet to act?
   You'll need to fold quite a few more hands.

5. When else should you be slightly more apt to fold?
   If your opponent is in early position, if his bet is fairly large, or if you yourself have a fairly short stack.

6. What is the best time to make this call?
   When your stack is large, your short stacked opponent is on the button or in the small blind, and when you are in the big blind.

The Gap Concept
Doesn't Always Apply

1. Are there times when it is wrong to abide by the Gap Concept?
   Yes.

2. When does this occur?
   When the players in the pot have a lot of chips compared to the blinds.

3. When is this especially true?
   If you are a no-limit expert.

4. When such is the case, what should you often do?
   Call a moderate raise pre-flop with hands that are obviously worse than what you think the raiser has.

5. Examples?
   You might call with king-nine suited, eight-six suited, or even jack-ten offsuit.

6. What is the reason for making these calls?
   The dramatic advantage which accrues to you when you have position on your opponent, especially if you are an expert at playing big stacks.

7. What if you are against an opponent who may be afraid of damaging their stack?
   Your positional advantage may be even greater than a normal ring game. This means you may be able to profitably play even more hands.

When Chips
Don't Lose Value

1. What are two examples of when chips sometimes don't lose value?

When you are not at a good table or you are not that great a player.

2. What if you don't think you have a nice overall edge on your opponents?

Then there is no reason to pass up any edge that does come your way, at least not in the beginning or middle stages of the tournament.

3. What if a great player has a very small stack?

He no longer has plus EV with those chips.

4. What if you have two possible bets where the upcoming bet is a bad bet but yet is one that you must make and the first bet has a somewhat negative EV.

You should make the first bet.

5. When does this typically occur in a no-limit hold 'em tournament?

When the blinds are coming up, there is an ante, and you have a short stack.

6. How small does your stack have to be before you fall into the situation where chips don't lose value?

An estimate would be between 15 and 30 times the big blind.

How Amateurs
Should Play the
Deep-Stacked Early Rounds

1. What strategy should great players use?
   They should be cautious early on.

2. What about weak players?
   The opposite is normally true.

3. Why?
   Their edges won't accumulate, and they are less likely to recognize better opportunities in the future.

4. What does this mean?
   These players should be willing to risk lots of chips with any slight edge, especially if that involves putting pressure on those great players who are trying to avoid such confrontations.

5. Is there an exception?
   Yes.

6. What is it?
   At the beginning of large tournaments when the stacks are deep, great players should play quite liberally.

7. Why does this work for the great players?
   Because they are not risking *large* amounts of chips with small edges.

8. But what about the less than great player?
   The normal rules also reverse for him.

9. Why?
   Since he cannot outplay his opponents for a large amount of chips in comparison to his stack, he shouldn't gamble at all.

10. What problem does he have?
    If he gets involved with marginal hands, he still has lots of chips on the later rounds.

11. So what is the bottom line?
    If you are a decent tournament player and understand the theories presented in this book, but you are not that good a cash game player, you should consider playing ultra tight if you are at a tough table those first few rounds.

Sit 'n Go Tournaments

1. Do the principles of tournament play apply to sit 'n go's.
   Yes, even more so than to a normal tournament.

2. What is the main reason sit 'n go's are different from normal tournaments?
   There is a giant jump in prize money from fourth to third.

3. What is extremely strong in the late stages of a sit 'n go tournament?
   First-in equity.

4. What is highly related to the strength of first-in equity?
   The Gap Concept.

5. What does this mean?
   The greater the importance of that equity, the bigger the gap between the raiser's requirements and the caller's requirements.

6. What does the giant prize for third place do?
   It leads one to a survival strategy especially in the early rounds.

7. What does this mean?
   It is wrong to push small edges in a sit 'n go, especially if you are calling someone else's bet.

8. What is another reason to play the initial stages quite tightly, especially when it comes to calling?

By making big gambles with small edges you may lose out on being able to make similar gambles with bigger edges later on.

9. Why will you have bigger edges later on?

You understand the concepts related to the late stages of a sit 'n go and most of your opponents will not.

10. What is more likely to be correct in a sit 'n go than a normal tournament?

The play of "checking it down" with an opponent when there is a third player all-in.

11. When is this especially true?

When the all-in player can bust one out of the money.

Questions and Answers

Afterthought

Again, these questions are not designed to replace the material in the text. Their purpose is to help keep you sharp between complete readings of *Tournament Poker for Advanced Players.* I recommend that when you believe you have become a proficient tournament poker player that you read the text material every other month and review the questions about once a week. Also, remember to cover the answers and to think through those questions that you have trouble with. In addition, attempt to relate the questions to recent tournament hands that you have played, and try to determine which concepts were the correct ones to apply.

Conclusion

As we have seen, at times tournaments are very different from normal poker games. It's no wonder that some people who excel at them do poorly in the standard ring games and vice versa.

It all starts with the prize structure and how the chips change value. Of course, the Gap Concept comes into constant play. And whether you have a short or a large stack, or whether your opponent has a short or a large stack, can dramatically impact your decisions.

And tournaments can really become interesting when there are just a few people left. Much can change on the turn of a card and some of our World Champions won their titles when they got lucky and drew out on that final hand.

But always keep in mind that tournament poker is, despite its differences, a form of poker. This means that you must be very skilled to achieve a high level of success. Those players who attempt to "fire away" almost always discover that they run out of chips, and those players who just try to survive, almost always discover that they didn't have enough chips.

Remember, when you're broke, you're done, and the same is true for your opponents. This fact dramatically changes play from a normal poker game and frequently creates a large Gap that you must exploit. Also, keep in mind that unnecessary, close gambles, even when you have the best of it, can be terrific mistakes in tournament poker, while the exact same plays produce much of your long term profit in the side games. Also, keep in mind that many of the tournament concepts we have talked about are relatively unimportant early in an event, but can make all the difference once there are only a few people left.

Yes, tournament poker can be a lot of fun, and these events can occasionally produce a big score if you are fortunate enough to win a large one. But they also require much skill, and being a successful tournament player requires much more than luck even though the luck factor can be very large in the short run.

In closing, I hope you found this book to be everything you expected, and I'll see you at the final table.

Index